Dedication

This book is dedicated to all the amazing people in the world who often feel invisible, the little girls and boys struggling to find their voices, and those who feel like rock bottom is the only foundation they have. Healing takes time, patience, and a level of commitment that I was once fearful of discovering. This journey will not be easy but it will be the greatest journey of all.

THE BATTLE
Within

KRISTINA QUARLES

www.TrueVinePublishing.org

The Battle Within
Kristina Quarles

Published by
True Vine Publishing Co.
P.O. Box 22448
Nashville, TN 37202
www.TrueVinePublishing.org

ISBN: 978-1-956469-31-8 Paperback
ISBN: 978-1-956469-32-5 eBook

The book you are about to read is based on a true story. Some names and identifying details have been changed to protect the privacy of individuals. Any names similar to individuals related to or who may personally know the author are strictly coincidental.

Cover photo by Motelewa Smith Photography
www.Motelewasmithphotography.com

Printed in the United States of America—First Printing

To buy more books or to book author for speaking engagements, contact. www.KristinaQuarles.com

Acknowledgments

There are no words that will ever describe the gratitude I have for the overflowing love and support my family, friends, and publishing team have shown me during this process. You believed in me when I didn't believe in myself. I don't know where I would be without all of you!

A special thanks to my beloved husband. You have stood by my side through every twist and turn, never wavering from the bond and commitment we made to each other. You are my very best friend, my backbone, my rock, and my foundation. Thank you for believing in me, loving me, and making me see how strong I have always been.

To my amazing children, you are my inspiration and motivation to push through every obstacle that comes my way. You have shown me the beauty in every storm, the sunshine in the darkness, and the joy behind the sorrow. You are the light of my life.

Introduction

We often second guess our decisions, blame ourselves for undesirable outcomes, and wish for the chance to reset our lives. However, we are not the authors of our own stories! If we were, everyone would be happy right?

At least those are our thoughts anyway. If it were up to us we would all be rich, have perfect relationships, the desired number of children, no sickness, and no suffering. But in that world, none of us would understand the true meaning of love, empowerment, or appreciation. With love comes pain and out of pain a stronger, more meaningful love with lasting purpose is born.

I spent a lifetime searching for a purpose that already dwelt within me and I don't want you to do the same. My desire is that my story allows you to learn from my mistakes and fears. My hope is that this book compels you to open up your heart and be willing to heal before you are left feeling defeated, looking in the mirror one day fearful of the person staring back at you. When we endure pain, it creates anger and in an attempt to shield our brokenness we put on a mask to hide our hurt from the world!

I want you to be able to look in the mirror with the understanding that you are remarkably made with a purpose greater than you could imagine, and you are not alone!

You are not the result of any negative circumstance that has occurred in your life, and you deserve to have people in your corner that celebrate the fact that you are a big fucking deal! Refuse to settle for less!

Don't be ashamed of your past! We all experience wrong turns and rough terrains in our lives. We must be willing to climb every mountain, stand in every storm, shoot past the stars, and never give up in order to identify our purpose, experience victory, and learn from our journeys.

Life can be a wonderful maze of growth and overflowing aspirations if we allow it to be. Trust the journey you are on even when you don't understand it. Find peace in knowing that in your darkest times you are not alone, believe you are worth fighting for.

Let's go on a journey together. A journey of pain, resentment, and loss, so that we can discover the true meaning of life, and the power of loving ourselves!

Prologue

"Why?" I muttered, eyes still closed and head hanging low.

"I don't know!" Dan responded.

My heart raced faster and faster as a lump filled my throat.

"Are you kidding me!? I deserve an answer. WHY??"

"I don't know. I don't remember that night the way you do. Do you really think I raped you?"

My whole body began to shake, covered in goose-bumps, my blood literally boiling!

"Are you fucking kidding me!? There is no way you believe I wanted this! That I wanted my life and spirit ripped from my body! Do you really believe I wanted to live in fear, never trusting anyone or anything, questioning every decision I make in life?"

"I don't see that night the way you do. I am sorry that you think I did something to hurt you or something happened that you regretted after the fact!"

I jumped from my chair in a rage, fists tightly closed, heart beating so quickly it could be seen through my shirt!

"You DON'T deserve to breathe! You have taken everything from me!"

I could feel my rage taking over. I was going to hurt Dan. If I could have killed him right there, I would have.

"Calm down Kristina" Blue-Eyes screamed.
I was losing control of myself. How did I let it get this far? I hate the person he made me!

***

Have you ever stopped and thought, I can't do this anymore? Has the pain ever been so intense, that you struggled to breath? Have you ever longed for something so much that you could not stand? Have you ever found yourself surrounded by people, but still felt alone?

These questions seized my thoughts and occupied my dreams for years, stunting my growth and hindering my ability to love. I soon found myself consumed with a world full of stereotypes and over suggested expectations, which quickly led me down a very troublesome road, struggling with self-identity. I never quite knew where I fit in, and always found myself living in the shadows. The lonely truth is that many young boys and girls are struggling with self-identity like I was , but it doesn't have to be!

Thoughts of insecurity and hurt plagued my existence, crippling my steps, clouding my judgment, and misguiding my path until I was finally brave enough to accept them as my truths and face them head on. Let's take a deeper look into my pain, the demons that lay within, and the secrets untold!

Broken Pieces

"I am stronger than I think, smarter than I know, and capable of more than I will ever imagine."

–Unknown

I grew up in Michigan, raised by my stepfather and his family, who always loved me as their own. My two older siblings and I are from my mother's first marriage (we are all French, Canadian, German, and Polish) and to the naked eye we look white. My younger siblings are biracial (white and black) and from my mother's second marriage to my stepdad, the only dad I truly know. My stepfather also has three children of his own from previous relationships. We are a family of thirteen total: five girls, and six boys, along with mom and dad. We were a real life Brady Bunch, although our life wasn't as fun loving as the family on T.V.

In my mind, memories of my childhood are like broken and shattered pieces of glass. I have flashbacks of certain events from earlier memories but cannot quite put together all the pieces. I am the third child, and youngest of my mother's first marriage. My eldest brother is six years older than me, followed by my older sister who is four years older than me.

We did not get to see our biological father much growing up due to his illness and distance. Unfortunately, I never knew the healthy version of my father. He was diagnosed with Huntington's Chorea when I was very young. Huntington's is a rare, genetic disease that causes a progressive breakdown of the nerve cells in our brain. The sprinkled memories of my father consists of a very slender man, long dark beard, hunched stance, slurred speech, curly hair, with the prettiest smile and eyes you have ever seen!

My older brother, Stewy, was my father's twin, minus the curly hair. Sadly, my earliest memory of Stewy was also of him being sick. He inherited Huntington's Chorea from our father. He was eleven when he was diagnosed so I was far too young to understand what was happening. As time passed his demeanor began to diminish. He would shift from the fun loving, playful brother that I adored to a manic, confused child searching for an outlet to escape not only the pain on the outside but the pain on the inside. At times he would get so angry, his eyes would almost turn black. It was like you could look through his soul. Watching him sit in the room and rock back and forth, with a blank stare, and no words was hard to process as such a young girl. I hated seeing him that way and didn't want to accept that this is who my brother was. Although he never said he was sad or upset, he was sick and like anyone who cares about their siblings, I just wanted to fix it for him!

I always admired my older sister, Tiffany. She was tall, thin, with very long, dark brown hair. At first glance, her hair looked black. It was so silky and shiny like a cat's coat. Her eyes were big, and bright, with a stunning shade of emerald green. I wanted to be just like my big sister, I was definitely her shadow! She and I were extremely close. She was my protector and always let me tag along with whatever she was doing.

I don't have many childhood memories of my younger siblings, I just remember spending time with my great-grandmother (on my mother's side of the family) as our immediate family grew. During holidays my older siblings and I would go to my mother's side of the family, while my younger siblings got to spend every holiday with Mom and Dad. It was as if the house was divided.

Part of me felt like I was being pushed out of my family. My parents seemed to be preoccupied with my younger siblings. As time went on, we seemed to be in two different groups conducting separate lives. My older brother Stewy was becoming sicker with each passing day, more frequent mood swings, aggressive behaviors, and tantrums that made it difficult for us to help him. Ultimately resulting in my brother going to live in a group home, dividing the two groups even more.

Stewy would come home for the holidays and weekends but as a child, I felt like I lost my brother. In my mind, he was discarded and separated because he was different. At the time I did not understand the depth of his mood swings or how they could negatively impact our younger siblings. My lack of understanding left me confused with feelings of rejection and abandonment. As my younger siblings grew, the attention shifted to them, and I was left feeling isolated. With Stewy gone most of the time, and Tiffany getting older and staying out more, I couldn't help but see my family differently now. A loving family that was once all circled together, had now pushed me off to the side, left to figure out life alone, forsaken by all to find my own happiness during a time when my mind was full of imagination and a growing desire to be seen.

My parents were complete opposites. My dad was loud, funny, affectionate, giving and always the life of the party! My mother seemed quiet and distracted most of the time, never really engaged with my day-to-day activities. Dad was the only parent that worked outside of the home until I was in high school. I watched him come home every day, the routine was like clockwork. He'd burst through the door, this tall, stocky man with deep chocolate skin and a baritone voice, "I'm home." He would announce as he came through the door from work. He was always happy. His deep, unforgettable voice would fill the house with joy. He was always telling some stupid joke that made zero sense but would always have us rolling with laughter.

"Where are you getting this stuff from, Dad?!" I would scream, letting out a deep, powerful laugh that came from the pit of my stomach, stealing all of my breath and bringing me to tears.

With a huge smile hidden under his scruffy beard, he'd lean down and kiss me on the forehead and say,

"How was your day blue eyes?"

There was nothing I loved more in this world than those special moments with my Dad. In a sense, the longing I had to know my biological father pushed me closer to my dad. My connection with him seemed to help fill the void for all the unanswered questions I had related to my father.

While I was enjoying the time I spent with my dad, I seemed to be losing more of my mother every day. As the needs of my younger siblings grew, my mother became more preoccupied with taking care of them and less invested in having a relationship with me, pushing me ever closer to my dad. It didn't matter if he was going to the gas station to get beer, going to play the lottery, or going to get weed, I wanted to go. The bond we had made me feel less abandoned. When I was with my dad, I was important, I belonged, I was part of a family. I was daddy's little girl when we were together, and no one could take that from me.

As I began to drift even further from my mom, feelings of alienation and thoughts of not being good enough created an enormous wedge between my mother and I, which made it impossible for us to build a real relationship. I couldn't fully understand why I pushed her away so much or why I never told her how I felt. I was young and deluded and wasn't sure that she would care. My thoughts of what a family should look like and how a mother and daughter should bond did not match my reality.

With time, I started to realize that I blamed her for leaving my father, pushing me aside when my siblings were born, and not showing me that I was important. Every time I was in the room, it was as if the energy was being sucked out by a vacuum cleaner. No matter what the atmosphere was before I walked in, it would always shift in the most awkward way. Maybe it was because I was in dire need of attention and mom always seemed too busy to be bothered with me. It didn't take long before my mind convinced me that I was a burden and needed to take care of myself.

Maybe I remind her too much of my father. Maybe she is scared I will get sick too, so it is easier to push me away, I would presume. My thoughts would send me into a whirlwind of assumptions, trying to figure out why I couldn't get the same amount of recognition as my siblings.

Nothing I did seemed good enough. Each day mirrored the one before it: full of criticism and reminders of all my mistakes. Somehow, even that seemed better than being ignored. Things were so different with my dad. I could tell him anything without judgment or thoughts of insecurity.

Dad was the only person in my bubble that loved me for me, or at least that's how I imagined it at the time anyway. No matter how busy he was, he always found time for me and my older siblings. He never made us feel like his "stepchildren." Anything he did for one, he did for us all! Some of my younger siblings will tell you he did more for the three of us than for them. It was almost like he could sense the need for extra attention and went out his way to fill the void.

Even with all of the love my dad showed me, I still felt a part of me was missing. Dad and my older sister were the only people at home who seemed to care to be around me. My mother and her family had several differences which made it nearly impossible to build a true connection with them. My only lifeline to my mother's side of the family was my great grandmother Helen.

Tiffany and I spent a significant amount of time with Grandma Helen, but only saw my mom's extended family on holidays. Mom and her family were estranged. It was never talked about much growing up, but it was clear they did not agree with my mom marrying outside of her race.

I did not really know my biological father's family except for one uncle. The differences my mother had with them seemed to trickle over onto the three of us, preventing a relationship from being formed at all. The relationship between my mom and my biological father is very cloudy, the only piece that remains clear is the resentment I held for her leaving him in his time of need. The rest of the pieces seemed insignificant compared to my longing desire to know the other half of me. With each passing year, I found myself in a game of tug of war, desperately seeking an identity that fit in all aspects of my life.

What must I do to make my mother's family love me and want to be part of my life? Why does Mom love my younger siblings more than me? What do I have to do to make her see me? WHAT DO I DO?

Standing in the bathroom each morning, I found myself drifting off into the eyes of my reflection, searching for something unknown–something I would not find until much later in life. I wanted to know who the person was behind my reflection, only if she had the answers I was in need of.

As middle school approached, the atmosphere in the house seemed pretty consistent. Dad was still the life of the party, so we all looked forward to him coming home. Our house always seemed full of people and noise, everyone talking over each other, T.V. playing in the background, and kids running in and out of the house.

As a child, I simply thought my family was loud. Dad especially, seemed very expressive and obnoxious. Every conversation seemed to echo through the house and bounce off the walls. It wasn't until I was a little older that I realized, the loudness was just the pain, pushing its way through all the barriers put in place to hold it in. With time the loudness could no longer disguise itself as just conversation, it was finally being revealed as the constant and consistent turmoil it truly was.

Everything in our house was a debate, an argument, and more times than not a one-sided conversation. Our talks that started as healthy dialogue, often ended in unresolved disagreements due to the steadfast unwillingness to hear each other out. The older I got, the clearer the picture became. Our house was just a roof and walls, with food and furniture, lacking consistent love and sustainability. Our house would never be a home!

It's funny how we believe the barriers we construct in our lives will protect us, yet somehow we always remain in a constant state of war—an internal fight that becomes stronger and stronger with time, until we find ourselves looking for any way to throw in the white flag. Sometimes the pain gets so intense and the future can be so uncertain that surrender seems like the only option. Accepting my family's loud, chaotic nature as normal was so much less painful then acknowledging the dysfunction as the consistent disruption that it was.

Welcome to the
Real World

August 1991, *Middle School here I come!*

The first day of school was at hand, and I was overwhelmed with excitement and nervous all at the same time! I was finally old enough to make my grand entrance into middle school and I could barely contain myself. My days of being a little kid were over and I was looking forward to seeing what life had to offer. I tossed and turned, fighting to get comfortable, but my mind would not let me rest, flooded with thoughts about what the morning would bring. After drifting off in my imagination, I finally fell asleep only to wake up in what seemed like moments later. Bursting with exuberance, I jumped out of bed tossing clothes all over the closet before I noticed the moonlight through the bedroom window.

What time is it? I thought to myself as I dashed to the alarm clock sitting on the nightstand.

"4 AM!" I shouted as I plopped back down on the bed in frustration. There was no going back to sleep now!

Aggressively turning to the side, I grabbed my pillow, glaring at the alarm clock as if my staring could force the time to change. "Come on come on, be time already" I said in frustration. Getting ready too early meant playing the waiting game but I suppose there was no way to avoid the wait... So, that is exactly what I did. I waited and waited and... waited.

Before I knew it, the time lapse was over, and my alarm was echoing through the room. Beep!! Beep!! I jolted out of the bed as if someone forcefully pushed me. Jumping right over my blanket I made my way back to the closet in search of the perfect outfit.

"Tiffany!" I screamed, calling for my sister. "Tiffany!"

"What girl? Stop yelling, you will wake the dead!" She said.

"What do girls in middle school wear?" I asked, as I folded my arms demanding she answer me.

"Just be yourself! Everyone will love you!" She responded as she pulled me in closer, messing up my hair and laughing.

I spent a lot of time overhearing my older sister talk about middle school. It always seemed like such fun with all the sports and the band performances. It was like I was stepping into a new world full of mystery and adventure. I must have changed my outfit five times before picking the right one, which for me, was my favorite jeans and a shirt.

Who cares what you look like? Stop worrying the day is going to be great! I thought to myself as I rushed down the steps.

I fumbled through the kitchen cabinets and opened the refrigerator door a million times in search of food. *You can't eat. There is no time!* I thought to myself. Finally giving up I went back to my room to double check that I had everything.

My stomach was in knots and not just because I was hungry. I couldn't stop thinking about how the first day of 7th grade was going to go. One of the girls next door, Jamie, who was a little older than me, met me at my house and we walked to school together. Although I was nervous, I tried my best to laugh it off and play it cool! Jamie tried to calm my nerves by telling me how her first year of middle school just flew by, but it was only making it worse.

"There is nothing to worry about. The hallways and classrooms are always so loud you won't even know what is going on. Just try to focus on your work!" Jamie said with a smile.

Why is it going to be so loud?? I thought to myself, starting to panic. *Is everyone just having fun or are the teachers not paying attention??* Thoughts of curiosity were driving me insane. Come to think of it, my loud upbringing may have prepared me for this.

It had been roughly 20 minutes and it felt like the Great Monarch Butterfly migration was happening in my stomach the entire walk to school. By the time we got there, I thought I was going to throw up!

We arrived at the two-story brown and burgundy brick schoolhouse. Children were running everywhere with school buses lined up around the front and side of the building. Old school friends were greeting one another, happy to reunite after the long summer. The voice of yelling teachers trying to gather the children into the school rang from all four corners of the building. I quickly realized that middle school was very different from what I had pictured in my head. The school was so big and some of the kids seemed much older and mature than me.

I'm never going to be able to find my way around here!

Trying hard to mask my nervous jitters and just be myself, I pushed my way through the crowd of unfamiliar faces. Tears nearly fell down my face when I found out that my friends from elementary school would all be separated and sent to different homerooms. Now I was left to face this unknown world solo.

***

The first few weeks of school seemed to fly by. I kept to myself most of the time, not speaking much in class unless I was spoken to. I wanted to break out of my comfort zone so I could make new friends, but it was much harder than I anticipated. Everyone seemed so grown up, all the girls wore makeup and tight clothes, all the boys wore their pants low and spent a lot of time hanging out at the lockers.

Struggling to find my words and interact with people was a new challenge for me. It never seemed like the right time to introduce myself and if I did what was I supposed to say? I found myself going to the bathroom several times a day, checking my clothes and obsessing about my hair. But no matter how well put together I was, saying "hi" to people in the hallway was either met with a laugh or them rolling their eyes. Participating in class now made me a teacher's pet or a nerd. What I thought would be an adventure turned into a confusing cluster of emotions in a matter of days. In an instant, the perception I had on life came tumbling down all around me.

Middle school was not the beautiful, exhilarating place I had envisioned at all. Instead, it was a place full of stereotypes, pressure, bullying, and pain. This once shy, bright, blue-eyed girl, with long curly hair; was starting to notice that maybe she didn't fit in at middle school either. With the snap of my fingers, reality set in, displaying a distorted picture with broken lines, faded images, and a bent frame.

The real world is not a nice place, and there are expectations everywhere you go! Everything I once thought was beautiful about me, made me an outcast from everyone else. My skin was different, my hair was different, my eyes were different, the way I walked and talked; everything about me made me stand out in the worst way. I seemed odd and my differences highlighted the fact that I didn't belong. I was being introduced to the real world and it presented a new meaning of ugliness!

I grew up in a multicultural home, very aware of different races and cultures, but the color of our skin did not matter to my family. The man who raised me, and who I loved most in this world was a black man. My skin color was obviously different, but never a factor that impacted my life, until I got to middle school that is. Race and skin color was never a topic of conversation with my family but it was now clear the rest of the world wasn't as comfortable with it as we were. Everyday that I went to school was like turning on a light switch that left me shining brightly in the middle of the room. My skin, something I never paid any attention to before, turned into a focal point for my existence, placing a cloud over me that seemed to follow me everywhere I went. Was I white, was I trying to be black? Why did people feel like they needed to know my race and why was my skin color such a big deal. I didn't want it to be a big deal, I wanted to fit in or at the least fade into the background, but I wasn't able to do either.

I started to hate everything I saw in the mirror! I started picking myself a part like the kids at school did until I wasn't able to find anything beautiful about myself anymore.

Why am I so different? No one is ever going to like me!

My mornings turned into a nightmare with my clothes thrown all over the room and my dresser covered in hair products that I didn't know how to use. My attempts to dress differently were met with ridicule from other girls.

"Look at her! She is too skinny to even wear that!" Girls would laugh and point as I walked down the hall

I hung my head in frustration trying to figure out what in the world was wrong with me! I even went to the extreme of cutting off all of my hair, praying I would no longer stick out like a sore thumb. My once long, light brown curly hair, was in a short uneven dark brown, bob. Looking in the mirror just added to my anger. I immediately wanted my long curls back.

What did I do?? This is crazy! I thought, banging my fists against the sink.

"Come here little sister!" Tiffany said from the other room. "Let me help!"

"There is no point. I look so dumb. I have made everything worse!" I said in defeat.

"No, you didn't! Just give me a few minutes little sister!" She said with a smile. Like a scene out of a movie she began tugging my hair left and right. Dust went flying through the air as I closed my eyes and hoped for the best.

"Okay! Go look now." Tiffany said with excitement.

I slowly walked to the bathroom, trying to think of a way to convince my parents to let me stay home. Entering the bathroom, I ducked down in fear of what I might see. As my head slowly moved up towards the mirror, I could not believe that was me staring back!

"Oh my God! How did you do that?! I look so different!" I shouted.

"No, you don't! You are still you and you are beautiful! Now get ready for school before you get in trouble." Tiffany said as she left the room.

As I searched the room for something to match my new look, I was in awe of the new me my sister created. The curling iron worked like magic and the makeup brush was like pixie dust, as they worked together to magnify all the features I once loved about myself.

I walked into school with a new attitude that morning, my head was held high and I had an extra bounce in my strut. I was surprised as a few boys took their time walking past my locker and even said good morning. Before I got a chance to bask in the moment, my confidence was quickly disintegrated as a girl I never seen before walked up to me as I was closing my locker.

"Are you kidding me? Who do you think you are?" She asked in disgust.

"What?" I responded in confusion.

"Just because you change your hair, and your clothes does not make you black. You are still a stupid little white teacher's pet that doesn't belong here!" She said bumping into me as she walked off.

"Go back to Kansas little girl!" Her friend shouted down the hall as they disappeared around the corner.

Feeling completely defeated, I rushed to the bathroom and washed my face. Trying desperately to remove the makeup and undo all of Tiffany's hard work that had me feeling like a brand-new girl just moments before.

They are right! I am never going to fit in! I thought, scrubbing harder until my face was red. *Great, now I look like a clown too! Fuck it!*

Walking to class, I paid attention to every detail of my classmates' clothes, their hair, the way they interacted with each other, even the way they carried their books.

I am not that different! I thought. We were all girls, all had hair, and clothes, and none of us were really exactly the same. So why were my differences so important when we all had our own unique features and characteristics. For the life of me I just couldn't figure it out.

Fashion, makeup, shoes, and trends never crossed my mind until then. Suddenly these topics were the center-piece of my existence. *Even my friends* would make fun of my off-brand clothes and shoes.

"Girl, why are you wearing those buddies?" they joked.

"What's wrong with my shoes?" I would ask.

"Girl we can't be seen with you wearing those cheap ass shoes! And untie your shoelaces, stop walking around looking so stiff!" they would say.

We were living in the era of untied fat-laces and ankle socks with the fuzzy ball on the back with white shell-toe Adidas. Still naive enough to believe trying to fit in was going to fix my identity crisis, I raced home full of toxic energy.

"Mom, can I get some Adidas?"

"Some, what?" she asked in total confusion.

"I hate these shoes. All of my friends are making fun of me." I blurted out.

"Fuck what those kids think!" Dad belted from the room, "stick up for yourself. You don't have to be like them. All that matters is what you think!"

I wanted so badly to have the strength and "don't care attitude" my dad had. But I could not see past the embarrassment of being bullied and the shame of my friends not wanting to be around me. Growing up in such a big household there was no way my parents could afford to get me new shoes, so my aunt gave me a pair of her Reeboks. Even though Reeboks were not as popular as Adidas or Nikes, they were name-brand enough to be "cool" or at least that is what I hoped.

Gone were the days of long flowing dresses, baggy pants and tee shirts. I needed to show my figure, that is what all the popular girls were doing. I spent hours in the mirror trying on clothes, picking through Tiffany's things, and cutting the bottom off of my shirts so I looked older. Soon all of my clothes were tighter, and my closet was full of form-fitted pants, bodysuits, and short skirts, and crop tops. Everything that showed how small my waist was and how nice my hips looked were my go-to outfits.

I tried to fit in a little more by listening to popular music, discovering Mary J, SWV, Xscape, and Eazy E. I remember learning every word to Xscape's *Understanding*, I even practiced the dance moves in the mirror. No matter how much I tried to be like everyone else, there was always another flaw waiting to be discovered. Becoming a teenager can be a hard journey for anyone, mix in a little bit of family dysfunction, lack of self-confidence, and extreme pressure to fit in and you have the perfect disaster waiting to happen.

Going to school became a tormenting rollercoaster ride! What do I wear? Who do I talk to? and how do I respond when a boy gives me attention?

***

"Hey snowflake!"

Two girls were standing at their lockers. I had never heard that term before, so I didn't stop walking.

"Hey snowflake!" they yelled again.

Still puzzled with confusion. I assumed they were joking.

"Are you talking to me?" I said with an innocent smile.

"We better not see you talking to Bee, no more, you white bitch." One of the girls threatened.

My smile dropped. Bee was a friend from my neighborhood. I had known him longer than I could remember. *Where is this coming from?* I wondered.

My body was trembling with growing aggression. I wanted so badly to say something back to them, but I was frozen in place as they turned and laughed. My anger filled stares could have burned through the back of their shirts, as I watched them walk to class.

I wish I could say the bullying ended there, but I'd be lying. It seemed to intensify with each passing day, resulting in rising hostility. I was so confused!

I am too white! I am not cool enough and now I can't be friends with a boy!?

My attempts to fit in worked in a sense, they gained me attention from the wandering eyes of boys and daggering glares from girls.

How does any of this make sense? I thought.

The bullying seemed to be mostly related to girls who were purely jealous about boys. But some of it was related to race, these bullying attempts hurt the most. I didn't judge anyone for the way they looked, dressed, talked, or walked. I couldn't fathom how such a large group of my peers disliked me based on appearance when none of them knew me and weren't willing to get to know me!

"Damn! You smell like a wet dog" they would mutter.

With me ignoring the threats regarding my friendship with Bee, he remained my listening ear, but he was never around when the comments were made. He was my only comfort. His responses to my explosive venting remained consistent, always trying to cheer me up with compliments.

"You know they are jealous of you because you are so smart and have everyone's attention, don't give them what they want. You are better than them." He would say.

"Am I? I sure don't feel all that special." I would respond.

"Trust me, someday you will see what I see." Bee would reply.

Even though one of the girls antagonizing me was Bee's girlfriend, he never avoided me and would even walk me to classes if he was around. Besides Bee, I had no other outlets. Home should have been my safe place, but it couldn't because there was too much dysfunction and pain there. With the non-stop fighting between Mom and Dad, home resembled more of a battlefield than a place of peace and rest. The fights would grow in intensity until Dad left or passed out drunk, or Mom would simply try to defuse the fight by going in the other room.

I quickly realized "brushing things under the rug" was mom's way of dealing (or not dealing) with the issue.

Just walk away from it and it will go away had become my mantra. As long as I could keep everything swept under the rug no one would be able to see the mess. My head was throbbing, robbing me of the ability to focus. Raging frustration, unexplained emotions, and no clue how to deal with any of them was making my heart slowly turn cold. I was full of anger due to the bullying, which soon turned to anger towards myself.

"Just stick up for yourself. They are not any better than you." I would say to myself, but never say out loud.

I spent most of my time standing in the mirror taking mental notes of everything wrong with me; drawing imaginary lines to map out all the changes that needed to be made; flipping through magazines fantasizing about what "perfect" meant. Luckily my phone rang while I was giving myself yet another inspection of my flaws.

"Hello" I said in a disconnected tone, still focused on my reflection in the mirror.

"Hey. What are you doing?" Bee asked.

"Oh, just reminding myself of all my imperfections!" I replied.

"Stop being silly! There is nothing wrong with you." He insisted.

"Of course there isn't. I just need to change everything about myself." I said.

"Well, I think you are perfect the way you are. Stop worrying about everyone else!" He exclaimed.

"Thanks. You have to say that you are my friend!"

"Whatever!" He said, dismissing my negativity.

Bee and I had been close for a long time, but something started to feel different when we talked. My heart skipped a beat when the phone rang, hoping it was him. The excitement I used to feel when I saw him at school, shifted. There was no longer a sense of relief when he came around, although he had always been my saving grace, it had become more a feeling of warmth. The butterflies grew more every time he came around. I would even find myself laughing when he didn't say anything funny.

Keeping my eyes on him as we talked became more of a struggle, feeling like his gaze was exposing how I really felt about him. I became discombobulated when he looked at me for too long and even started blushing when he smiled. When we hugged hello, the squeezes seemed tighter, I was melting in his arms like hot wax. Our embraces lasted longer than ever before, and I had no objection.

"What is happening? He is like a brother to me." I would think to myself, sighing as I walked to class.

All my focus started to drift, daydreaming in class became more frequent, and lingering to see him in passing started to be a daily occurrence.

You too have been friends forever, and he has a girlfriend that hates you. I would remind myself every time I got close to him.

With so much tension at home, there was no time for my silly teenage crushes and battles with self-identity. So, I just continued to hold strong on the battlefield, all alone, holding in all of my confusion, frustration, anger, and unexplained emotions. However, the battle didn't stay contained for long before the war started again.

The inner war would come and go. Sometimes I could suppress it, other times I would surrender to it, but I could never win it. My dad wasn't able to comfort me the way he did when I was younger. It was like his words of encouragement and life became a soft whisper against a group of people whose hatred for me rung loud and clear. I could see his concern for me, and it was evident that he didn't understand why I refused to stand up for myself and let how others felt affect me. I didn't understand it either.

Between the bullying and my escalating feelings towards Bee. I didn't know whether I was coming or going. There was a part of me that wanted to cry out to my dad. To just get in his lap and pour out my heart, but my teenage pride wouldn't let me. I always wondered if my biological father was anything like me growing up, or if he was a no-nonsense type of guy like dad. I couldn't help but consider that maybe his reassurance or presence growing up may have been the thing I needed to now feel okay in my own skin. Maybe knowing him in some way could have helped me to know myself.

Saying Goodbye to a Love I Never Knew

*D*ark curly hair, bald on the top, full beard, unforgettable laugh, and breathtaking smile. These are the only memories of my biological father that remain. I was a baby when he became sick, the memories of our time spent together are just a glimpse into a lost existence.

Stories of his temper and willpower were shared with love, reminding me that he was strong, determined, and not willing to give up! However, the unconditional love he so proudly wore as a gold medal, also had a dark side. As I got older the affection found in these stories faded as pictures of all the physical abuse my mother endured by his hands came into focus.

My mind grappled, trying to make sense of it all, confused more at the thought that the two men I loved most in this world hurt my mother. How could this man that I longed to know, longed to find a remote piece of resemblance to be so cruel? I instantly started to pick out parts of my mother that would cause the man I envisioned to turn cold.

There is no way my father could do those things. I wish I could ask him. Why would she ever tell us that?

The more I focused on the unknown, trying to complete a puzzle with several missing pieces, the more my frustration and anger towards my mother grew. Too afraid to ask her for details, I allowed my imagination to grow wild with the assumption and reasoning of whatever my 13-year-old brain could conjure up.

Her name is tattooed on his arm!? He still smiles if we bring her up!? This just doesn't make sense!

My adolescent mind couldn't seem to process the lingering confusion or find the right words to say to my mother. I took a note from her lesson book and brushed all these emotions under the rug with the rest of my trauma and pain. *Ignore it and it will go away!* Or so I thought. In reality I just continued to build resentment towards her. Mom was moving on with her life, leaving my father behind to suffer in sickness by himself.

When she left him, I am certain that a part of me, stayed with my father. A part of me still had more questions than answers and wasn't able to walk away as easily as my mom did. Pushing me completely out of the family, my mom built a new life with my dad and younger siblings. It seemed as if she was trying to erase every piece of her life before Dad and I was caught in the crossfire– a painful memory of a past life, a love lost!

***

As our father's illness grew, my aunt and uncle became our lifeline to him. They tried their very best to make sure the three of us spent time with our father. My uncle made it his priority to make sure we had some holiday memories with him. Tiffany and I used to reminisce by looking at old pictures and scrapbooks, . The photos of my father and Tiffany's memories were all I had to cling on to. The more I flipped through the photographic pages of his life, I grew angry with myself for not remembering him, not holding those moments close to my heart!

I wasn't even that young! Why can't I remember?!

His condition continued to worsen, eventually leaving him bedridden or confined to a wheelchair, alone all day. My aunt went out of her way to make sure the three of us were able to remain part of my father's life until the very end. She would take us to see him in the nursing home as time allowed. Sadly, I was too young to remember the majority of these visits in detail. Just as my holiday memories, I am left with only pictures and stories of how much he loved his family.

I was intrigued by the fact that no matter how sick my father looked, he was always smiling! I often wondered what thoughts triggered his happiness and why I found it so difficult to do the same. The only memory of my father I wish I could erase from my mind completely is our last trip to the nursing home!

As we approached the nursing facility, everything seemed so old and everyone so distant. We slowly walked down what seemed to be a never-ending hallway. A combination of odorous smells filled the air as my little eyes wandered from side to side, peaking at all the patient's we passed on the way to Father's room. His bedroom door was slightly cracked open. The sounds of the screeching metal from the door being pushed open reminded me of nails on a chalkboard.

I turned my head to the left, standing slightly behind Tiffany, anxious to see Father but nervous of how his condition may have progressed. He was sitting almost completely straight, propped up in bed with pillows and covered in a white sheet, as his smile pierced through his dark, full beard.

"Hi dad", Tiffany said with excitement.

"Hi dad!" I said immediately after, not giving him enough time to respond.

A look of confusion filled his face as he attempted to adjust his body in bed and muter a response.

"That is Tiffany and Krissi." My aunt responded.

I wasn't sure what he said or even if she understood him, I just knew the look on his face cut me to the core, like a dagger through my chest. He no longer recognized me!

I ran out of the room in tears, ashamed that I was unable to cope with the changes in my father's appearance, speech, and mental decline. He looked so sick. Much sicker than I ever remembered from our previous visits. I sat on the floor outside of his bedroom door, so many thoughts racing through my head.

"Come back in the room honey, your father knows you are here, it just took him a minute to realize who was in the room." My aunt said as she wrapped her arms around me and whipped the tears from my eyes.

I slowly stood up, fixing the floral print shirt that grandma made for me, just to wear for him. Holding my aunt's hand, we walked back in the room together. Hesitant to look back towards the bed, I slowly lifted my head. To my surprise, I was greeted by my father's bright, warm smile that I loved so much. I'll never forget how beautiful and infectious it was.

***

The sound of the back door slamming and my book bag sliding across the kitchen floor, hitting the chair, is all I heard as I rushed in the house from school.

I instantly noticed my aunt and Mom sitting on the couch. Mom's head was hanging low, face beet red, with my aunt sitting next to her with her arm wrapped around her shoulder. "Mom!" I said in confusion as I walked towards the living room.

"Mom, what's wrong?" I asked as I quickly rushed to her side.

In that moment, all of the built-up aggression and frustration I had towards my mom was pushed to the wayside. She seemed to be in so much pain and as her little girl, I just wanted to take it all away. I slowly walked over and stood in front of her, trying to decipher why her heart was so broken. I reached out my hand as mom lifted her head, making eye contact for a moment. My eyes filled with tears seeing the growing pain in her expression.

"I need to talk to you and your sister. Please sit down honey!" She whispered.

The air in the room seemed to get thicker with each passing minute as we waited for Tiffany to get home. Mom was quiet as we all sat anticipating Tiffany's arrival. I was unable to gain control of my nerves. Anxiously shaking my legs, I tried to divert my thoughts. I had no idea what was happening. My aunt was never over this early and by the solemn looks on both their faces, I knew whatever it was had to be bad.

Wait! Where is Dad? Oh my God, is something wrong with grandma? I wondered.

It seemed like hours passed as different scenarios pierced though my mind like hot bullets. Every scenario was more horrific than the next, as I tried to read the thoughts behind the agony in my mom's eyes. As my sister walked in, my mother motioned for her to come into the living room with us.

"What's up?! Why is it so quiet in here? Where is everyone?! Tiffany asked.

Mom cleared her throat and took a deep sigh. "Girls, I am so sorry!" Pausing as she gathered the strength to finish her sentence, she forced out her next words in a low voice as tears ran down her face. "Your father passed away."

"What?" My sister said as she was overtaken with emotion.

"When? How do you know?" I replied, standing to my feet.

"When the nursing home could not reach anyone by phone, they sent a letter to your grandfather's house. Girls, I am so sorry!" Mom cried.

"I don't understand! When did he die? Was he alone? When did you find out?" I cried out in despair.

"We don't have all the answers girls but listen to me please! You cannot tell your brother. He is too sick and will not be able to handle knowing your father is gone." Mom begged.

I just stood still, trapped in the unbelievable truth that my father was gone. My mind was spinning in circles. Struggling to hold the tears in, all I could do was stand there. Growing confusion and this unfamiliar aching pinch in my stomach began to swallow me whole. Mom looked so broken. I was reeling with emotions, I couldn't tell if she was hurting for us or because her first true love was gone. Although they had been separated for years, there was such an indescribable look in her eyes as she told us he passed. A look of emptiness, completion, and fear all wrapped in an ugly, miserable bow.

Maybe she cared about him more than we knew. She never gave off that there were any feelings left for him but her reaction in that moment communicated something different. Her first boyfriend, her first husband, and the father of her first three children was gone. She hadn't seen him in years and now she would never get to say goodbye. It was hard for me to imagine the extent of her pain all while still having to watch her first born son get sicker with each passing day.

The one door that left so many unanswered questions was now permanently shut. I felt selfish for being sad and couldn't find the words to even respond. Turning my body away, I slowly glanced back at mom just in time to see her head drop down again. I ran upstairs to my room and plopped down on the ground in front of my bed and cried. I cried about missing all the moments that I couldn't remember, all the moments that would never come, and all the questions that would forever go unanswered!

"We are going to be okay Kris, dad was really sick." Tiffany said, sitting on the floor next to me.

"I know, but we didn't get to say goodbye." I cried. "Do you think he was sad? Do you think he was in pain?" I asked.

"All you need to know is how much our father loved us and only wanted us to be happy, he would not want you sad. I promise." She whispered in my ear as she held me close and played with my hair. Twirling small, individual strands around her finger as she rested her head on top of mine.

"How am I supposed to feel?" I asked.

"I don't know, but we will figure it out together. I will never leave you. I promise." She answered, as she kissed my forehead.

Lost in bewilderment, I had to find the strength to say goodbye to the love I never knew. 1992, Stewart James Wilcox, died alone, in a nursing home roughly an hour from where we lived.

I stood in front of a full length mirror in my bedroom, examining my face, searching for features that resembled him. Rubbing my hand along my jawbone, playing with my hair, smiling and frowning, dissecting each part of me desperately hoping to see a glimpse of our father in the mirror!

Falling to my knees, taking a deep, exhausted breath, I felt defeated and lost. Nothing else mattered, not school, boys or bullies. Nothing could quench my pain, and nothing hailed in comparison to my heartache. So many unspoken words, so many questions, so much hidden fear. My heart was literally ripped from my chest that day, almost 30 years later, I still have not managed to find all the pieces.

***

By the time our father passed, my older brother, Stewy, was already diagnosed with Huntington's and Tiffany was starting to show signs of this very unforgiving disease. The pressure of life's unrelenting grasp was too much to bear. I had nowhere to turn, no one to talk to. I was alone trying to reconcile the exit of someone from life who never made a formal entrance.

How do I say goodbye to someone I don't really know? How do I process the sorrow? How do I heal the pain without looking weak? How do I move on without being bitter with the world? How do I forgive my mother for leaving him when he needed her the most, for not taking me to see him, for not making sure I knew his side of my family, for not going to his funeral with us, and most of all for sharing the bad parts of him with me? How do I move forward without fear that this disease will claim me as its next victim? How do I forgive God?!

Saying goodbye to someone is never an easy process, whether it is simply growing apart, or losing someone completely. Grief can show itself in a variety of ways and travel down different roads until we feel healed enough to let go, or at least move on. This process requires strength and emotional support to maneuver through the journey grief takes you on. When we neglect the grieving process and fail to allow ourselves to go through these emotional steps, we risk falling into depression and feelings of guilt.

Each wall was inching its way closer to the center of my room, the light dimming, as I curled up in the fetal position in the middle of the floor. It felt like the room was collapsing down on my small body! My 13-year-old mind was spinning out of control, trapped in a nightmare, no alarm clock to wake me up. I couldn't talk to my mother, she didn't seem to care or was too preoccupied working through her own emotions!

I couldn't talk to my dad; I didn't want to be a burden on him and had no clue how all of this was making him feel. He is the one who had always been there and now we were all grieving the person he so graciously stepped in to compensate for. I couldn't talk to my older siblings, I couldn't even imagine how they felt being that they had more memories with my father.

I couldn't talk to my younger siblings; they were just too young to understand and protecting them from these types of emotions was my role as the big sister. I only had my so-called friends, and Bee. I stared into space, questioning God, and praying for healing in the same breath. I was willing to do or try anything to numb the pain...

Numbing the Pain

I spent countless nights sitting in my room, silently crying so no one would hear the pain I endured. With each passing day I felt more of myself being pushed into hiding, determined to find an escape. The pressures of school, bullying, and changes in hormones began to increase as the death of my father added an extra weight that became unbearable.

I began waking to cold chills which did not result in the normal reaction of reaching for a blanket. My mind jumped to panic,

This is the first sign! I have Huntington's!

The thought of developing the same sickness that took the life of my father instantly choked me up and resulted in tears! I would have to force myself to lay down, focus on an isolated part of the ceiling and drift away. There was no one to console me; no one to calm my fears. There was only me, being held captive to the imaginations of a tormented teenage mind. I became hyper-attentive to the smallest movements. Afraid of what the days to come would hold, I watched my feet as I walked to make sure I wasn't stepping too high.

One of the first things I noticed in my siblings is that their perception of space, height, and distance was distorted. I became fixated on my movements. Studying Tiffany and Stewy's behaviors, the way they walked, talked, even the way they ate became an obsession of mine. I began fearfully comparing their movements to mine, reversing the prayers from previous years, now begging that we do not resemble each other at all.

"This is crazy, all you have ever wanted was to be like her!" I would say to myself in tears, looking in the mirror. "God please hear me! Why won't you help them?"

***

As I was dealing internally with all of these challenges, I was watching Stewy become sicker. Everything about the big brother I once knew was changing right before my eyes. It seemed like overnight that he was not able to walk, and his tremors were worse with each passing day. Visits home started to dwindle down, weekend visits turned into once a month, which soon turned into mostly holidays. Walking with handheld assistance, turned into him being pushed in a wheelchair, and eventually being picked up and carried from the car to the house by our dad.

My big brother was six years older than me! He helped me learn to walk, feed myself, taught me to play hide and seek and always let me win! The brother that was supposed to scare boys away and teach me to fight, was fighting for his life and back to wearing a bib and diapers. He was soon unable to feed himself or even lift the silverware, which eventually became plastic wear out of fear he would hurt himself. Everything was moving so fast, yet I couldn't move past who my brother was to accept who he had become..

Tiffany's ability to walk was now starting to diminish. First, her steps became slightly off balanced, resembling that of a person highly intoxicated. My loving, bubbly, carefree sister suddenly had a temper. Growing up, Tiff would cry if you killed a bug, but the young woman that was standing before me was full of rage and anger. She was willing to fight anyone if she didn't get her way, including me.

Would this become my reality? The sister I grew up with was becoming a stranger that I was fighting to recognize and there was nothing I could do to help her!

Nothing seemed real anymore. I was living in an alternate universe where the worse was always happening and hoping for the best was setting yourself up for disappointment. I grew hesitant to say goodbye when Tiff and I would leave each other, never knowing what the next day had in store for us. My soul was screaming for an outlet, something had to change and quickly!

***

Bee was trying to help but it is hard to help someone when you are just as broken. We had been friends since the second grade, but he never really talked about what happened at home, he was just always looking for a reason to leave. He became my only listening ear, but jealous girls continued to add fights to my battlefield. Soon my one listening ear was not enough.

I had more on my plate than I could manage and was growing tired of the bullying and name calling! I was starting to hate those miserable girls making comments and bumping into me as I walked down the hall. It would always make my blood boil but now I wasn't sure how much longer I could contain it. There were moments where my skin literally felt like it was crawling with rage. My fire was growing stronger and stronger with every passing day. My heart turning ice cold, prayers not being answered, festering more anger towards God. I could feel a monstrous storm brewing deep inside my soul and I knew if I unleashed it there would be no turning back!

With nowhere to run or hide, searching for any sense of relief my inexperienced eyes soon resorted to the one place I often looked to find answers. Back to my bedroom mirror, staring face to face with my inner demons, with bloodshot eyes, and my hands trembling with fear for the future I wondered once again. Who am I? Was there more to me than what I knew or was I only the sum of what I had experienced thus far in life? Tears poured down my face as I thought of burying my siblings, longing to see my father again, worried that the rage I was feeling was not simply grief but an early sign that Huntington's was knocking on my door. I opened a bottle of vodka I took from my grandmother's house, stared deep into my blue eyes and turned the bottle up. I could hear my tears hitting the glass. With each swallow the vodka seared my throat and chest like acid, but I just kept drinking. Praying with each sip the pain would disappear!

What do I have to lose?

Alcohol became my listening ear–a secret source of reliance that quickly sent me spiraling. I don't know if my family was blind, or if I was just invisible but no one seemed to notice the tailspin my life was in. At school, I had been labeled a whore who was trying to steal everyone's man. If someone was feeling very generous, they would remind me that the boys were only talking to me because "they know all white girls are easy."

"You are so stupid, you silly white bitch! He only wants you for one thing!" Girls said in laughter as they saw me talking to a boy in the hallway.

I was reaching my breaking point quickly, so full of anger I would feel myself shake with rage. How much can one person take?

"Keep pushing me, and you are going to get exactly what the fuck you are asking for!" I calmly said back, as they walked past.

"What did you say little girl? Is that a threat?" One of them responded.

"It can be a threat or a promise, you decide but I am done playing these games." I quickly responded, bumping into one of them as I walked past.

Alcohol was giving me courage, a feeling I had never known, the power to fight back! I was so proud of myself, I finally did it, I finally stuck up for myself. I was so excited to get home and tell my dad what happened.

"Dad!" I yelled as I ran in the house, but I didn't get a response. Dad had already left to the liquor store and was headed to my aunt and uncle's house. There was a note sitting on the table, telling me they would be back. Still full of adrenaline I sat at the kitchen table, tapping my nails, allowing the sound to soothe me. I was excited about this newfound feeling, finding it hard to stop jumping up and down inside knowing that alcohol was my secret weapon. I called Bee over to celebrate my bravado.

The basement was Bee and I's safe place when we hung out. We were able to blast our music and drink in peace without the rest of the world taking notice. My parents were usually gone pretty late into the night and never came downstairs.

"I'm proud of you Krissi!" Bee said with that smile that took my breath away. "But you know you're better than that. Are you really going to let them turn you into a bad girl?" He asked jokingly, but I knew he was serious.

"I am so over being the good girl." I yelled. "It's getting me nowhere. I hardly have any friends, because I am either too white or trying to be black. If I talk to boys, they accuse me of trying to steal someone's boyfriend. Fuck them! One of these days I am going to just walk up and kiss one of their boyfriends in front of them!"

I took another sloppy, drunken swig of my drink; the alcohol dribbling down my chin. Bee walked up closely and gently wiped my chin dry. Everything got quiet as we gazed into each other's eyes. All of a sudden, everything else faded into the background and it was just he and I, with only the sound of my pounding heartbeat filling the air. He gently leaned in and kissed me,

"You are better than all of them." he whispered.

My body went limp. I was like a wet noodle trying to regain my composure. Heat surged through my body as I stood in utter shock at how passionate our kiss was.

What are you doing? I thought.

I was scared of crossing the friend zone line with him but felt so connected to him at the same time. The house was quiet, like everything stopped in honor of our first kiss. The music seemed to fade out and go silent as my heartbeat got faster and louder. I had never kissed anyone, never experienced the feeling flowing through my body, the buckle in my knees, or the lump in my throat. Bee had always been someone special and in that moment our platonic friendship died as I embraced the desire for him to be something more. He was one of the only people I felt truly loved me for the person I was and now was my chance to release the pent-up feelings I had for him.

He pulled my shirt over my head and rubbed his hands down my back, a warm sensation quickly sent tingles through my body. The room faded to black and the only thing on my mind was Bee. The magnetic connection I felt with him brought all the negativity in my life to a screeching halt as my clothes continued to come off. Layer by layer and piece by piece all my flaws and insecurities became exposed. I was embarrassed to show my body and continued to cover my chest. I wouldn't even change in front of my mother, now I was standing completely nude in front of my best friend. Although uncomfortable, something about it felt right. Here I was baring it all in front of the one person who always saw the beauty and best in me regardless of what anyone else saw or didn't see.

What are you doing? This is Bee? I continued to repeat to myself, but I couldn't stop. I just wanted all the negativity around me to wash away!

"You are absolutely beautiful, inside and out. Promise me you will never forget that!" Bee whispered as he slowly kissed my neck.

For the first time in my life, someone had seen *all of me* and still found me beautiful. He looked at me with pure adoration, without judgment of any sort. I shared my first kiss and my virginity all in the same night. We made love and then laid in each other's arms for hours. No talking, no drinking, just me wrapped tightly, intertwined in his arms and legs, with music softly playing in the background, numb of all hurt and pain.

Taking Control

Clothes flying around my head, alarm clock blaring until I yanked the cord out of the wall, tossing a broken hanger on the bed, struggling to force my leg into my jeans and blow my hair out of my face at the same time.

"What did you do?" I repeated to myself in a panic as I rushed around the room getting ready for school. Part of me felt loved, the other part of me was upset for giving away my purity.

Oh my God! What did I just do? The only thing I had left was gone, tossed away on a spurt of vulnerability! He was my person, he had a girlfriend, I was so broken, a million reasons to say no and a million more pushing me to him. The tender moment that felt right the night before, now felt wrong for so many reasons.

My once best friend became my lover...but he wasn't. We were a hidden secret from the world, his girlfriend adored him, and we had just spent the last several months convincing everyone we were just longtime friends. Or maybe we were trying to convince ourselves. Either way, I had done something that I could never take back and I wasn't sure that I wanted to. I was so angry with myself for being reckless, and thinking one stupid night would not spiral my already destructive world into a disastrous tornado. The only person I trusted, now viewed me in a different light. I could not help but think that every time he looked at me, he didn't see his friend looking back anymore.

Does he really still care, or am I just a piece of ass now? I couldn't help but wonder.

Even in my brokenness I fully understood, once you cross that invisible line that defines friendship, there is no turning back. One moment of intoxicated bliss shifted the small piece of happiness I was clinging on to. All the time spent trying to convince others that we were friends was so much easier than listening to him sell his girlfriend a make believe story of love and commitment, knowing that he had laid with me and we shared something far more special than anything they could ever have.

Was our friendship less than I imagined? He couldn't really love me. How could I be so careless with myself and the only relationship that mattered? These thoughts would continue to penetrate my mind as I searched for a way to make sense of it all.

No matter how scattered and demeaning my thoughts got, I could not stay away from Bee. The closeness I felt around him made the confusing emotions worth it somehow.

Everyone calls you a slut who is trying to steal their man anyway, so why not? I said, with a shrug of the shoulders, giving myself a devilish wink in the mirror.

The rumors became true, and I was now everything they said I was. My bitterness and loneliness finally succeeded and completely overtook me. I could have never imagined that for years to come I would allow these overwhelming feelings and hidden pain to set limitations on my happiness.

***

Jealous girls are very mean creatures, vindictive, manipulative, identity crushers. Walking away only works for so long before the disgruntled mind plays tricks on you and somehow makes you believe one decision will not alter the rest of your journey. Bee and I continued to have our secret rendezvous in the shadows for several months. My parents never questioned the time we spent together, and why would they? It was just Bee!

But everyone else started to notice the changes in our interaction. The way my eyes sparkled when he said hello, the way our hugs seemed more intimate each time we embraced. How we stole glances of each other in passing and became unknowingly flirtatious with each other. As the rumors gained momentum, I started to pull away from Bee because unlike before, they weren't just rumors this time. I still couldn't get over how I allowed my damaged heart to cloud my judgment. I was never really sure of who I wanted to be but I knew this wasn't it.

We tried hard to remain friends, or at least he did but things were never the same between us. A hug was never just going to be a hug again, saying I love you before hanging up the phone took on a whole new meaning. There was no way to go back to the buddy I met in second grade. Too many blurred lines, too much pain! Hanging out with him at my house was no longer the free-spirited experience of friendship that it once was. As he left my house one night, I held tight as if I was losing him forever.

When we said goodbye I held on to his hand as he went to walk away, hesitant to let go. He turned back and smiled, squeezing my hand before releasing,

"I will call you later, love you!" he said.

I just nodded my head and smiled back, watching him walk down the street knowing this goodbye meant something different to me than it did to him. I had to let him go. I couldn't allow my pain to hurt someone I loved so deeply. I was just too hurt to pretend to be the friend he once had. Pretending felt more agonizing than just walking away from it all.

As the rumors continued to gain fuel around the speculation of me and Bee's relationship, the bullying began to get physical. I was at the point of no return, so I just laughed in the faces of mean girls while saying hi to their boyfriends just to rattle their feathers. Of course, this started a wildfire that quickly burned out of control but hey... I was a can of damaged goods with no regard for others as this point. Girls clearly felt like they had something to prove, resorting to placing things in my chair, knocking my books off my desk, whispering, "theirs that cracker white bitch", or yelling, "you blued-eyed devil", as I walked past.

"You are never going to belong here, no matter how hard you try, you will never be black!" One girl muttered, as she pushed her way into a seat between me and someone else at the lunch table.

A burning sensation started in my toes and slowly creeped up my legs, as I stared at her with a blank face, waiting for one of my "friends" to say something. Anything at all to defend me. *Complete silence.*

The girl stood up and started laughing. My so-called "friends" didn't say anything. By the time the burn reached my fingertips my mind just went blank. As I stood up my mouth began moving before I got a chance to think.

"Do you think I give a FUCK, what you think of me?!" As if I was talking in a megaphone my voice rung across the lunchroom with power and assertiveness that I had not possessed until that moment.

The cafeteria remained quiet while everyone looked in shock, waiting for a fight to break out. My eyes stayed locked with her eyes, no words, just an empty, haunting stare. She chuckled and nodded her head leaving the cafeteria. I stood patiently still and focused until the sound of the other kids laughing broke the silence in the room. Pushing my tray out of the way, I walked off.

"Wait Krissi! Where are you going?" One of my friends shouted.

I just kept walking! Mind completely made up. They were not my friends.

Who the hell does that? No one said anything!

The following day housed tension from the lunchroom escapades as I noticed I was being followed to class. *Enough is enough.* I resolved.

For the first time, every emotion, every negative thought, all the pain and frustration came rushing out through physical aggression! This intense sense of release came over me. The adrenaline flowing through my body had enough force to bring the entire school crumbling to the ground!

"Do you think I don't realize you are following me?" I turned and asked four girls who were trailing close behind me as I walked up the steps to the second floor.

"And if we are following you, what the fuck are you going to do?" One girl mocked.

"She aint gonna do shit but run home to her mommy." another chuckled.

"I am so sick of this SHIT" I yelled, as I threw my books down on the ground.

Before I knew it, I had grabbed the girl with the loudest mouth by her head and started bashing it against a locker. Every thud of her head gave me the greatest satisfaction. Her friends quickly jumped in, but I didn't feel their attack. My adrenaline was overflowing. I was willing to fight all of them if I had to just to prove a point.

Kids in the nearby class came running out screaming in delight at the spectacle. "Fight! Fight! Fight!"

Teachers burst out of their classes, "Break it up! Break it up!"

One teacher grabbed me, struggling to get me to release the fist-full of hair in my grasp. I kicked and screamed, wanting to rip the girl's head off. As the fight was broken up, I reveled in joy at the scene. I felt the sting of the scratches and punches, tasted the blood running down my lip. It all hurt so good!

"Here Kristina, take this towel and clean your face!" Principle Matthews requested as she sat down preparing to call my parents.

"I don't need it!" I responded, sitting across from her with my arms folded, and a look that could kill.

I sat there, aggressively shaking my leg while she talked to my mom on the phone. Rolling my eyes with every, "yes ma'am", "we understand", wishing I could hear how my mother was responding. I was so frustrated, straightening my posture and sighing to gain Mrs. Matthews' attention,.

Just give me my punishment already! None of this matters!

Mrs. Matthews' sighed as she hung up the phone. "Kristina, your mother said she will talk to you when you get home. Please take this note and return to class."

I walked out of her office feeling so much lighter on my feet. Going straight to my locker in laughter, not caring who saw the bruises or blood on my shirt, they were my badges of honor. My whole face could have been blue, purple, and yellow for all I cared. The victory was in knowing I stuck up for myself. I was so anxious to hear my dad's response when he got home from work.

***

"Kris, what happened at school?" Dad said in a deep voice, as he walked in my room.

"I just couldn't take it anymore and before I knew it, I hit her. I don't even remember everything that happened." I explained.

"It's okay. I am proud of you! Next time, just let them hit you first," he said with a smile and wink as he walked out the door.

"Yes sir!" I responded, trying to stop myself from smiling because my jaw hurt so bad.

Getting ready for school the following week embodied a number of emotions.

What will I be called now? The crazy white girl?

"Fuck it! Let them think what they want to think!" I said to myself as I took one more look in the mirror and trotted down the stairs.

"Kris, do you want me to take you to school?" Mom asked.

"Nope! Whatever happens is going to happen anyway Mom!" I answered as I walked out the back door with a higher level of confidence than usual.

Walking to my locker that morning was odd, no one said anything to me, everyone just stared. At first I thought it was because I made zero effort to cover the bruise on my left jaw. Then I chuckled to myself, *they are not saying anything because they really think I am the crazy white girl!*

For the first time since starting middle school, I could breathe and felt in control. For my young, naïve mind, the answer was clear. I had to be a "mean girl". It was final, my mind was made up, the only person I could count on was *ME*! Someone else was born that day, and the scared, little insecure girl who wanted so desperately to fit in was gone forever!

"If it is a blue-eyed devil you want, then it is a blue-eyed devil you'll get!"

The Devil Appears!

My eyes turned red with tears, leaving a faded image of the girl I was. I'd had enough. The red that colored my eyes was filled with the pain of constant rejection, torment, bullying, and family drama that had taken its toll. My eyes told a story that lived deep in my soul. Each glance at someone heightened the intensity creating the color underneath; red with anger, red with regret, red with hatred, until something within me broke.

No more! The new me was taking over. A stronger me, that was not willing to compromise anymore, there was no time for bullshit, excuses, or second chances. "Kristina" was in control, holding all the cards in her hand and not giving a fuck what the world around her thought.

Holding the hand of the girl my dad called his beautiful "Blue-Eyes", escorting her to safety, far away from everyone's grasp. "Kristina" was charged with one job, to protect "Blue-Eyes" at all costs, even if it meant locking her away, forever if needed. Overcome with rage and a taste for vengeance I never imagined how long "Blue-Eyes" would have to lay dormant before feeling safe enough to resurface.

"Kristina" was a battering ram ready and willing to knock down anything that got in her way. The tears I once tried to hide from the world in embarrassment, I began to wear proudly as war paint. Alcohol had become my confidant, it was a great listener and confidence booster. This new, empowered version of myself, wasn't afraid of anything and gave me the courage to fight back. My feelings were protected, and my heart guarded, making it easy to not let people in and even easier to push the ones I once loved away. This newfound sense of control, power, and boundaries was all I needed, so I thought. I was bitter and vengeful, not to mention unknowingly vulnerable to the world around me.

Why should I be the only one hurting? Why should I be the only one feeling pain and confusion? I would think to myself in growing disdain. Standing in the mirror time and time again, with tears slowly rolling down my face as I lifted another drink to my mouth.

***

"Kristina" pushed everyone away, even Bee. When Bee and I saw each other, I preferred to drink more and talk less. Sex no longer strengthened my bond with him, instead, it created more distance. My whole mindset shifted. The world was cold and dark, and the only thing that mattered was protecting "Blue-Eyes" physically and emotionally. My spirit was drained of all positive energy.

Bee tried his best to be a source of positivity and affection, but I used him as I needed him instead of cherishing the bond we once had. As time passed it became so much easier to just place him on a shelf until I desired a shoulder to lean on again.

When leaving the house wasn't an option, I would lock myself in my room or in the basement listening to music and drinking to drown the sounds of Mom and Dad fighting out of my head. Once the alcohol wasn't enough or was gone, I knew I could call Bee. It didn't matter how much I pushed him away, he would always answer my call for help.

"Hey, you want to come over?" I would say in a low voice as he answered the phone. Anxiously anticipating his response due to me being so distant in the passing months.

"Anything for you. Are you okay?" He replied.

"Yeah, just going stir crazy over here. Mom and dad are not getting along, per usual."

"I am on my way. See you in about twenty minutes." He said, hanging up the phone.

Days, weeks, even months passed with me isolating myself. Even with our rocky relationship, partially due to my inability to "just be friends" Bee was always my shoulder to cry on, no matter what time of day or night I needed him. When things were too much to handle, he would sneak in the house just so I didn't feel alone. We would hide in the basement and drink until sun-up. Mom was going through her own period of isolation. She would often retreat to her room to be away from dad, who was passed out drunk and high. Depending on how bad things got, one of my younger brothers and younger sister would wake up and come downstairs with us.

"Sissy, are you down here?" echoed a little voice.

"Come here. You have to be quiet, remember." I would whisper as I pushed open the door to the basement family room.

"Hi Bee!" My little brother would say with excitement as Bee jumped up to hug him and swing him around in circles.

"Remember what your sister said, we have to stay quiet! So, what are we playing tonight?" Bee would kneel down and ask them with a big smile.

He would always make them laugh, tell them jokes, or play cards with them. As long as we stayed quiet, we could all enjoy a moment of peace and freedom without having to worry about what was happening upstairs or the aftermath the morning would bring. By this time, our relationship rarely consisted of sex, it was about pure companionship and a deeper form of intimacy.

The comfort I felt in his arms, the wholeness and understanding I saw in his eyes, the warmth I felt from our conversation; helped me bring down the walls just a little bit. In these times, we were each other's safety net. He knew he could say whatever to me and I would never look at him differently. His secrets were safe with me, and he provided that same security for me and my younger siblings, mainly one of my little brothers who thought he was the funniest person in the world.

Even if our basement bliss was only until morning, I felt loved and seen for the moment at least! A moment that would never last, and a feeling that would fade quickly as Kristina reminded me, feelings house weakness, and weakness opens the door for pain.

We must protect ourselves! We cannot move backwards especially for a boy that isn't even ours!

As time passed, I got used to the idea that Bee and I would never be together. I am certain, I helped fortify that reality by pushing him away and continuing to isolate myself. He never did anything to make me feel less than his girlfriend, and certainly never rejected me in public. Even knowing that it would create more tension between his girlfriend and him. Oftentimes he seemed to put my needs before hers, and even his own. The dynamic of our friendship was multi-dimensional. It was simple yet complicated.

"Hey, are you okay? I haven't heard from you in days." Bee said, grabbing my arm to gain my attention.

Slowly turning back to look over my shoulder, I had every intention of playing it cool, but his girlfriend couldn't help but sigh and roll her eyes, so of course I had to give her something to look at.

Trying to stop myself from laughing, I walked in close, licked my lips and raised my left eyebrow, giving just enough of a smirk to show my dimples.

"Hey, my love, I am good! I just needed some time to think, I will call you later." I said as I kissed him on the cheek and winked at her, walking away. Turning back one more time before bending the corner, "Love you!" I shouted in his direction, happily spinning back around, heading down the stairs.

To the world around me, I was becoming just another pretty, mean girl! As much as I desired it, underneath, I didn't believe I was worthy of unconditional love. I felt such a sense of emptiness, I couldn't help but convince myself that everyone else saw me that way too. With each passing day, I was becoming a master at pushing everyone away and building my walls as high as I possibly could.

Happiness is just an appearance, nothing real, nothing to mourn, nothing to seek!

The Spiral

*A*nxious to identify new ways to occupy my mind, I was eager to start working as soon as I was old enough. Being able to interact with people I didn't have to see around every corner seemed to be a positive adjustment for me. Laughter started to fill the spaces where negative thoughts thrived. Before I knew it, my time was consumed with two jobs. Working after school and on the weekends became part of my normal routine. Working allowed me to escape reality, and create the image I desired people to see, at least during my shift.

Cheeze's Pizza Extravaganza was the job where I spent most of my time. It created a healthy distraction for me. The sound of the birthday music and children running all around made me feel like a little kid again, free of all the pain and responsibility. I looked forward to being surrounded by fun for a few hours in my day.

"Hey Krissi, are you closing with us today?" One of my coworkers Penelope asked.

"Yeah!"

"Cool, we are going to have so much fun!" She chuckled.

I was hesitant at first, automatically thinking the worst.

Here we go with this mean girl shit! Now I am going to have to act crazy!

To my surprise, it was nothing like I imagined. Everyone was so much fun, running around the restaurant and playing hide and seek in the crawl tunnels. It was definitely a great change of pace. In no time, I had new friends, was going to parties, and making every effort to leave the frustrations from home and school far behind me.

***

"We say happy, you say birthday!" I shouted across the party room floor.

"HAPPY!" I shouted again, pointing to the birthday table with a big smile. Waiting for all the little smiling faces to shout "birthday" back.

A few coworkers and I finished our birthday dance in front of the stage, one of them dressed up as the mascot mouse Mr. Cheeze. I couldn't help but notice someone watching me from the corner table. I glanced back with an innocent smile, just enough for him to know I realized he was watching.

As the birthday song wrapped up, I headed towards the kitchen and off the showroom floor. Giving each child a high five so I had to walk past his table, making it impossible for him to not notice me.

"Excuse me ma'am." He said as I approached the side hallway.

"Yes, sir." I said as I glanced back to find him standing at the corner. I tried not to pay too much attention but there was something so appealing about him. Tall, dark milk chocolate, facial hair was so neat it looked like he drew it on. His voice was much deeper than I expected, intriguing me all the more.

"I was wondering when I was going to get to see you dance in costume for me?" He asked with a laugh.

"Really? You are very confident I see. Is it your birthday?" I asked.

"It can be if that's what it takes." He responded.

"I have to get back to work, but I am flattered." I said a bit shocked at his forwardness.

"Wait, what time are you off?" He asked.

"10pm. I am sure you will be done with whatever it is you are doing at a kid's fun center by then." I said jokingly.

"I don't mind waiting for something I am interested in." He responded

"Do you have a name, or should I just refer to you as mystery man?" I asked.

"Coi, but mystery man has a nice ring." He said.

"Hi Coi, my name is Krissi." I said as I smiled and walked away.

I finished wrapping the evening up and headed outside with one of my co-workers. We carpooled on our late nights. To my surprise, my mystery man was waiting outside.

"Did you really stay out here and wait for us to close?" I said with a suspicious look on my face.

"No, I left and came back." He responded, leaning against the hood of his car trying to act cool.

"I could have easily lied to you about what time I got out." I exclaimed.

"Not likely, you look pretty trustworthy," he said with a mischievous grin.

"Okay, you have my attention. Let's chat. I said.

"Do you drive, or can I take you somewhere?" he asked.

"I don't drive just yet; I won't be 16 for a few months. You can take me home and we can chat on the ride if you aren't scared I will kill you or kidnap you on the way." I laughed.

"I think that is a chance I am willing to take." he remarked.

"Are you sure you're okay girl?" My co-worker asked.

"Yeah, I am good!" I responded.

"Okay boy! I know what you look like, she better make it home!" She said to Coi, pointing at her eyes and then his, indicating she was watching me.

Coi just smiled at her and walked around the car to open the door for me. I just grinned watching him walk back around the front of the car. He had a little sway in his walk and a cute smirk as he tried to go unnoticed while watching me through the windshield.

The car ride started off quiet and I was understandably a little nervous. I slightly positioned my body to the side, with my weight shifted on my left hip so I was facing him, with my hand on my pepper spray. To my surprise, once we started to talk, the conversation was so easy. We talked like we had known each other for years. It felt good to laugh with someone that knew nothing about me, where I was from, or the depression I was struggling with.

"So, how did someone your age become so mature?" Coi asked, turning his head to the right to see my reaction.

"Unfortunately, a lot of pain." I quickly responded.

"Well, it is great to see that your pain hasn't completely taken that beautiful smile away. Trust me, I have lived through a little pain too and it is not always easy to smile." He said with the most sympathetic tone.

"Yeah! Sometimes it is just easier to smile and pretend the pain isn't there!" I said, watching his body language and facial expression, looking for anything negative I could find in him. Trying to anticipate the judgment and react to it before he has a chance to get under my skin. But there was nothing, no changes in his expression at all. We continued to talk, with him glancing at me every few minutes, smiling more each time. His energy made me feel welcomed and desired. I couldn't help but to smile back, while I was fighting off thoughts that he was just putting on a show to get me in his bed.

Girl he only wants one thing! I thought, as I tried to stop my eyebrow from raising in speculation of his intention.

When we made it to my house, he started to get out of the car, asking me to stay there for a minute.

"Okay!" I said in hesitation, as I noticed he was walking around to open my door.

"Why thank you!" I said with a smile.

"May I walk you to the door?" He asked.

"Sure!" I respond with a laugh.

He walked me in and introduced himself to my parents. This is something I definitely wasn't used to. As he reached his hand out to shake my dad's, I thought, *Oh my God please don't say anything crazy!* But Dad played it cool, he even offered Coi something to drink. We hung out and talked to my dad for a few hours.

For weeks, not a day went by without us talking, leading us into dating pretty quickly. There was a six-year age gap between the two of us. He was 21, no longer in school, working full time, had his own apartment, a car, and the freedom to move throughout life as he pleased.

I was 15 years old, forcing myself to stay in school, barely old enough to work, struggling with depression, developing a drinking dependency, and had only experienced one sexual partner in my life. Yet for such an age gap, our differences were balanced out perfectly. He was so easy to talk to and really seemed to listen. He didn't pry about my past and ask too many questions, we just lived in the moment. For me, this was the breath of fresh air I had longed for.

My parents adored Coi, it's like they were brainwashed into believing he was the perfect role model. Trusting him enough to pick me up for "school" in the morning, with the delusion that I was really going to school. The majority of the time, we would drop my little brother off at school and the rest of the day was ours to make the world around us disappear. I spent more time with him than school, work, and home combined.

Coi introduced me to a new world– a whole different crowd of people and a type of partying that I welcomed with open arms. Within a few months, I became a full-blown delinquent. This new dynamic, shifted the way I was viewed by everyone around me and started a new chapter in my life. A chapter full of drugs, excitement, danger, and more emotional pain than I could have imagined.

Every weekend was non-stop partying, with a few weekdays thrown in for extra fun. Coi's aunt and her friends always hung out with us, the house was never empty. There were only a few years between his aunt and him, so it was more of a friendship. There was never any drama though, always music, card playing, dancing, drinking, and drugs.

Coi would drink on occasion, but he never wanted to be around drugs. His aunt smoked weed sometimes, but her friends dabbled in a variety of substances, including pills. Up to this point, my drug of choice was alcohol. I saw my dad smoke weed, but I never tried it and wasn't familiar with any other types of drugs. However, the more I was around them the more curious I became.

***

I was so elated, getting ready for Coi's birthday party! Going frantic, picking out the decorations, snacks, and trying to make sure my outfit looked amazing! We never really went out because I was too young, so he was only used to seeing me in jeans or work clothes.

"You look stunning!" I told myself, smiling with excitement! Standing in front of the mirror, turning from side to side to make sure every angle popped out just enough. I took one last glance, adjusting my little black dress, and strapping up my heels just in time to rush out the door.

"Kris, Coi is here!" Mom yelled up the stairs.

By the time she finished her sentence, I was standing at the bottom of the steps, with a huge smile! "Happy Birthday baby!"

"Good lord! You look beautiful!" Coi said with a twinkle in his eye.

"Thanks!" I responded, trying not to look so happy or confident.

When we arrived at the house, I rushed in to help his aunt get everything in order before their friends began to show up. There were going to be several of his friends there I had never meet. I was worried about looking too young or acting too childish. The last thing I wanted to do was embarrass him. So, as the party got started, I made sure I mingled and took a drink when offered.

Sitting down to play cards, I noticed one of Coi's friends, Jack, crushing up some pills. "What are you doing?" I asked.

"Getting this party started. You guys want some?" Jack responded.

"No" Coi blurted out without hesitation. "We are good! Come on babe!" He said in a demanding voice.

"Oh is she your little puppy dog? Be a good girl and run along!" Jack said in laughter.

"Okay, when did you start answering for me?" I asked Coi, correcting him. "What do you have? Maybe I am interested." I quickly asked Jack, annoyed. I was worried about embarrassing him, but he was treating me like a child!

Coi gave me a disapproving scowl. I returned his look with an unfazed gaze of defiance. "Blue-Eyes" was gone. No one was going to control me, and I made sure Coi knew where I drew the line. He walked away shaking his head.

"More for us then!" Jack joked. Pointing to a small white pill, going on to explain, "This is Percocet. What you want to do is break it up and add it to the blunt or you can just snort it. It will change your life little girl."

Jack began to crush the pill with a spoon, until it was a fine powder. Scraping the powder up with a credit card, he carefully laced this marijuana and rolled the blunt. He was like a surgeon, the way he moved with such precision.

I was freaking out inside, but I wasn't going to let anyone in the room know it. Especially after getting so frustrated with Coi. I put on my bravest face, pulled my big girl panties up and acted like I knew what I was doing. Jack took the first drag of the blunt.

Cough!!! Jack began choking and laughing hysterically. As a big cloud of smoke circled around him. I thought he was dying, but he was laughing. He held out his hand with the blunt's glowing embers facing me.

Oh shit! My hand was shaking as I carefully pinched the blunt with my thumb and index finger–that's how I saw other people smoke weed and now was not the time to look like an amateur.

What the FUCK are you doing?! I screamed inside.

Pfff.. I took a huge toke! *Pfff*

"Slow down!" Everyone yelled and laughed at the same time.

I immediately felt like I was going to throw up and I had the most disgusting after taste in the back of my throat, like chalk. Dropping my head trying to maintain my balance, regretting my decision and praying Coi would come rescue me, I did my best to keep my composure.

"Sit down little girl!" Jack teased. He was so excited to see the drugs take effect. "Let that settle in" he giggled.

The party continued to go on without the birthday boy in the room. Laughter, music, puffing, and passing, while I sat as still as possible, waiting for the drugs to kick in. After about 10 minutes, I realized I couldn't stop smiling. I unwillingly started to sway from side to side in my chair, gripping the table with all my might as I tried to stand.

Gathering enough coordination to make it to my feet, I yelled "Bae"! Or I thought I yelled until I heard his aunt asking me what I said as she laughed uncontrollably. I just laughed, trying my hardest to walk towards the stairs, using the wall as a crutch to guide the way.

"Bae, come here!" I yelled far louder than necessary, making sure my voice could be heard this time! With my whole body plastered to the wall, I tried to correct my posture before he made it to me. Each step he made sounded like an elephant trotting towards water.

"You look silly. Why would you do that?" Coi was so upset.

"Okay, come on. I just want to live a little. Don't be mad baby!" I pleaded.

"We can live without all that extra shit." He said angrily.

"A little judgy aren't you? We were just drinking before we got here. I guess it is okay if you are picking the poison, huh?"

"Don't do that. It is not the same and you know it."

"But it is. Poison is poison at the end of the day. I am so sick of people trying to make my decisions for me."

"Well, stop making poor ones and I won't have to step in."

"WOW! I'm pretty sure you brought me around this shit and not the other way around." I said in frustration as I started to try and make it to the steps.

"Come here!" he said as he reached for me.

I quickly responded, "don't touch me! I can do it!"

"No, you can't!" He said in laugher, as he carried me downstairs and laid me on the bed to sleep off my high.

Jack was right. My life was changed that night. This new experience of weed and pills had ushered me into a world of ultimate escape. I had spent the last few years looking for a way to bury my problems and I had found it. As time went on, Coi became more unhappy with my drug use. I tried to slow things down for the sake of my relationship, but it was harder than I expected. It was like the pills were calling me and I couldn't help but answer.

Laced joints turned into popping pills, which soon turned into snorting crushed pills. I was quickly rolling down the hill of destruction with no one to stop me. Eventually the drinking and drug use was too frequent for Coi, and we started to drift apart. Although he never verbally expressed his opinion regarding my drug use after the first argument, it was obvious he was pulling away. I was wrapped up in the feeling the high gave me, I didn't do anything to try and hold on to what was left of our relationship at all. Just like Bee, I pushed him away.

Confused with the delusion that I had to be noticed by the opposite gender to matter, distracted by the sensation and relaxation of the drugs, determined to not be controlled, openly express my options, and never show vulnerability, I ultimately drove the people who attempted to display love and affection away, seeking attention from the people that held no real relevance to my journey.

The stereotypes I once despised now held me captive. The mean girl demeanor, the pretty face, tight clothes, and "fuck you" attitude portrayed me as the popular girl everyone desired to be around! "Kristina" needed no one, certainly not a grown man pouting like a boy! The chapter between Coi and I reached a close. No tears shed, not even a second thought, simply on to the next! *Popularity never looked so good!*

Ms. Popularity

Here I come, world! Full of energy, the center of attention, I had everything and nothing at the same time! A brand new me, or at least a new disguise... However, being popular isn't always what people make it out to be. I had my own money, made every room stand still, and grabbed the attention of every male when I walked in. Attempting to become an overachiever, I was involved in volleyball, cheerleading, soccer, the majorette team (short lived), and the track team; that one was even shorter! I tried everything to stay busy and fake a smile! In my mind, all these **distractions** made me blend in. My skin didn't stick out so much anymore, I was just one of the girls now. One of the popular girls, at least for the time being. Even with all this– with everything I thought I wanted– I wasn't happy, I wasn't whole, and still didn't feel loved.

My relationship with Bee was now nonexistent, I pushed Coi away, and felt like a ghost when I walked past my parents. I was becoming more confused with my identity and where to direct my focus every day.

I started to succumb to worldly pressures, growing feelings of doubt, and accepting that life simply sucked! Whenever I experienced times of weakness I tapped into the strength "Kristina" embodied, the resoluteness she possessed. "Kristina" allowed me to be confident, persuasive, and seductive. I no longer needed permission to have a good time and control the room! I had the world at my fingertips, and I was determined to enjoy the playground!

My last real conversation with Bee should have been painful but it couldn't be. My walls were built way too high and way too strong, making it impossible for them to be cracked even slightly by weak human emotion.

***

"Hello!" I said, answering the phone with a bitchy tone.

"Hey, I just wanted to check on you. You don't seem like yourself, what is really going on?" He sounded both concerned and agitated.

"What are you talking about? I am better than I have ever been." I responded, holding a drink in my hand, relying on my best friend, alcohol, to back me up for this conversation.

"You might be fooling them, but I know the real you. The loving and caring Kris, not this ice-cold person you are coming off as."

"Really? And who exactly gets to decide who I am? Are you proposing you have a say-so or do you need to ask your girlfriend?"

"Don't do that. I have never put anyone before our friendship, and you know that. Why do you keep pushing me out?"

"Are you serious? I am not broken anymore, and I can take care of myself. Why don't you go save your girlfriend?"

"I don't know what happened to you, to us, but you are not the person I fell in love with. I just want you to truly be happy, I want my friend back." He said, sadly.

"A few things to consider. There was never a "us". Our friendship died the moment you took my clothes off...The person you knew died a long time ago. I like this person better! I am stronger and protected. I was vulnerable with you and what did that get me? I was still second in your universe."

"I love you. I always have. This person you are becoming is not you!"

"This is ME!! This is who I have always wanted to be! You love the broken version, the shell of what I am becoming. Someday you will thank me for setting you free. You don't have to waste your time putting me back together anymore."

"I really do love you– all of you. I always have. I will be here when you decide to wake up. You cannot fool me with this act you are putting on, you cannot fool yourself either Krissi."

I felt my body starting to shake as tears rolled down my face, "Bye Bee." I said, knowing if I kept the conversation going "blue eyes" would try to resurface.

"Don't say bye. We promised we would never say bye. Bye is much too definite of an ending for us. Don't do this!" He begged.

"I do love you, but that love creates a weakness in me that I cannot afford to tolerate anymore. I don't want to hurt you. You deserve better than me and I deserve better than being second in someone's life!"

"Kris"

"Bye Bee. I do love you."

Overcome with emotion and a growing pain in my chest, I dropped the phone on the side of the bed. Slowly sitting down, glancing back towards my mirror, I prayed that "Kristina" was the one looking back and not a reflection that looked as pathetic as I felt inside.

My second real heartbreak, but this one I created all by myself out of fear. Fear of the one thing I thought I wanted the most. Fear of love, fear of getting it wrong, fear of letting him down, fear of not living up to this image he painted in his mind of me in second grade. Protection seemed like a double edge sword. On one end it cut off the pain, on the other end it also cut off the love. My innocence was shattered, and I did not plan on bringing "Blue-eyes" back anytime soon.

You are not convincing anyone you are happy, I thought as I stared into my reflection, too proud to wipe the tears from my eyes.

"Step your game up girl!" I told myself with a sigh. I forced a brave face, like a light switch being turned on as I blocked the thoughts clouding my judgment. I couldn't waste my time believing anyone cared for me, molding myself into the ideals of what someone else found suiting. So, the facade grew into an award-winning performance. I allowed myself to smile while the anger underneath thrived on the pain, rejection, and fear. I had created a monster who was willing to go to any length to keep others out.

You can change your hair, your friends, and get involved in as many activities as you want! Your parents still don't have time for you, and Bee is happy with his girlfriend, while you are faking a smile with anyone that gives you attention. Silly girl, you wasted so much time and energy on love.

Popularity was obviously for show, it didn't prove to be enough to erase the damage done, the words spoken, and the curse of me being invisible! While everyone saw Kristina, the real me was tucked away, safe in hiding.

How can everyone see me but them?! What the fuck do I have to do?

My parents didn't come to one game, it seemed like they didn't care about Blue eyes or Kristina. As long as I stayed busy, I could keep myself from caring. I never took team pictures, but I certainly never missed an after party–several of which were held at my house, knowing my parents would be at my aunts during the weekend.

My popularity was solely based on me being the life of the party! The once traumatized and hated white girl, was now the cool white girl with all the drugs, alcohol, and unsupervised parties your heart desired. Always smiling and laughing, with a twinkle in my eye, and down for whatever the wind blew my way. So alive to the world, but slowly deteriorating on the inside.

***

As children, we all want to grow up faster than we need to. We always want to be older, trying to fast forward time however we can. Wanting to prove that we can handle anything, aggressively pushing away any offered support or extended hands.

What we fail to realize is, we are *"children"* who require guidance and should not be forced to create distractions or transform who we are inside to fit into the world around us! Unbeknownst to us, the world would give anything to find its way back to the days of youth, we so desperately want to evade.

I, like many children in this world, lacked that guidance and sense of security growing up. The people I felt should have been protecting and guiding me, were ignoring and criticizing me. Part of me felt like I just wasn't important enough for them to care! I wanted to believe they loved me, and at times I felt like my dad went out of his way to make sure I didn't feel any different than my siblings. Other times, we fought like cats and dogs.

Some may say, this was a normal relationship for a teenager and her parents. It always amazes me that people are so quick to judge, so quick to pick a side, and determine what should have been normal for me, but would not survive walking a mile in my shoes! For that reason alone, my heart reserved the right to feel detached, lost, unwanted, and unheard.

***

As my partying grew, my dad's addictions were secretly growing as well. My dad's anger and pain were soon directed at the majority of the home, not just my mother. The courage alcohol gave me, ignited the fire in these arguments to blazing temperatures. In these moments I embraced being my mother's voice. Trying to protect her, fight for her, and gain her love in return. Sadly, the scene never played out in my favor. I was never hailed the victor, instead I was an out of control, disrespectful, lying teenager who only made matters worse! No matter how much I wanted to be the hero, all they could see was a villain.

***

"Are you kidding? I can hear you outside screaming at my mom like a toddler" I shouted with rage as I walked in the house.

"Fuck you, this is my house, and you are the child! Stay in your place" He responded.

Part of me was heartbroken, thinking to myself, *did he really just say, "fuck you" to me? The only person who is always in his corner.* My heart began to beat rapidly, eyebrows raised and eyes turning from blue to red with a devilish fury.

Thump, thump, thump; the sounds of my heartbeat grew with intensity, like a train racing down the track until I could no longer control my mouth!

"I am the child?! Are you 100% certain about that? I am working, helping you pay bills, and the only one that doesn't seem to run away from responsibility around here. So, fuck you!"

No longer afraid to speak my mind, the image of daddy's little girl quickly faded from the frame. Leaving only memories of the bright-blue eyed girl, running through the house with curls bouncing back and forth, racing to be next to my dad.

We were both rapidly changing for the worse, I cannot count the number of times I was told "I hate you" or "I hate you too" during an argument! One day, as I was sticking up for my mother, my dad decided to hit below the belt.

"Everything they say about you is true. You're just a little bitch like your mom!" He shouted.

"I got your BITCH" I screamed as I picked up the living room lamp and threw it at him.

"STOP IT!" My mom screamed out in tears, "both of you just stop it!"

My mother raced to the phone and called my grandmother, hoping she could calm my dad down. His mother was the only person he would listen to when his temper got out of control.

"Rick! Please come talk to your mom" Mom pleaded, holding the phone out with trembling hands.

Dad gave me a look as sharp as a blade and then he immediately changed his demeanor preparing to talk to granny.

"Why'd you call momma" he whispered to my mom while pointing the phone away.

"Ummm... Yes, ma'am... Umhm... But she... yes ma'am."

His conversation went on like this for a few minutes, and then "yes ma'am. I love you too. Kris, your granny wants to talk to you." He said in a shameful pout as he dropped the phone on the table.

"Yes, granny." I said, picking up the phone with full on innocence.

"Baby, you know your daddy loves you. You both just need to calm down and think about what you are saying. We did not raise you to disrespect your parents like that. Just give him time to calm down and you go in the other room. Everything will be fine tomorrow."

"Yes ma'am. I am sorry granny."

My granny always had a way of making the toughest situations seem hopeful. *Maybe she is right. Maybe this will all blow over in the morning*, I thought.

Morning came.

"Good morning, Dad." I uttered, hoping he was back to himself.

"Morning." He said, calmly.

"I am sorry, I don't hate you at all, I love you." I said in tears.

"I love you too, my blue eyes." He said as he kissed me on the forehead and walked out of the house.

This became our norm. My relationship with my dad had become a mirror image of his relationship with my mother. The difference was I would fight back, while Mom would cower. This spiral of drinking, drugs, and fighting became a normal, consistent part of life. So much, that I soon thought it was acceptable to be overlooked, pushed aside, and treated like I was second best. As long as the morning brought an apology, then we were supposed to just move past all the pain the words left behind.

The thing is, words can cut so deep and hurt for so long, there is no apology anyone can form that will truly make up for the scars left behind. The only time I felt in control was when I was drinking or getting high. Pretending to be happy became nature. I adopted the mentality that life was a never ending party, orchestrated by me! A party full of dysfunction, secrets, pain, bitterness, and addiction.

Craving the High

Power of Addiction

"Kris!" my mom yelled.

"One second." I responded frantically, scraping the crushed pills into a Ziploc bag and hiding the mirror in my dresser drawer.

Skipping down the steps, "yes ma'am?" I asked.

"The phone is for you!"

I talked to my friend for a few minutes, before hanging up and rushing back to my room to change my clothes.

"Mom, I am going to hang out with some friends, I will be back" I yelled, walking towards the back door.

"Don't you have to work?"

"Yep, we are just looking at speakers. I will be back in a few hours."

***

Drinking and getting high on the weekends started to turn into drinking and getting high every day. It didn't take long before being the life of the party turned my world into a tragic storm. Weed was now a thing of the past and Percocet wasn't enough by itself, soon being mixed with Vicodin and Xanax. Mixed drinks became less mixed with more liquor in each glass.

Sadly, when we suppress our emotions, hide our pain, and numb our senses, our judgment becomes increasingly cloudy. We tend to think everyone is our friend and there is no danger in having "fun". My clouded judgment became a filter over my eyes and ears that distorted the truth.

One lie, something I believed was innocent and necessary to avoid an argument and judgment from my mother, changed my life forever!

"Bye Mom", was the last she heard as I jumped into my friend Q's car, pulling out of the driveway before she could ask questions or see who I was with. We went to his house and headed straight to the basement. Everyone started pouring drinks and rolling blunts. We all laughed while the blunt was passed around. A few of Q's friends were debating about who could rap better, while I just laughed and joked,

"Neither of you can rap, so I am not sure what all the arguing is about."

Although I was used to being around a lot of guys. I started to feel a little uncomfortable as the house started to clear out, leaving me as the only girl in the room.

"Hey Q, can you take me home?" I asked nervously.

"Yeah, one sec. Come here for a quick minute. Let me show you something real fast". Q responded.

"Okay, hurry up, I have a lot to do before work tonight." I complained as I followed him into the room.

As I walked in the room, a very uneasy feeling permeated my soul. "Wha..." I could not finish speaking before I heard the door close, the metal of the lock turning. My heart dropped to the bottom of my stomach. Taking a deep breath, I turned around to face him. "What's up?" I asked, trying to force the anxiety out of my body.

"You know I have been checking you out, right?" Q asked.

"Boy please, it is not that type of party, and you know it!" I said, as the tension grew thick all around me.

"Stop playing hard to get", Q said as he pushed me on the bed and tried to kiss me.

I immediately shoved him, "What are you doing? You know I don't see you like that?"

"Oh come on, everyone knows you want it. That's the problem with you stuck up bitches, you want to party and want all the attention but no action." He said, moving in closer.

Panic seized my body. My adrenaline started to kick in and I began to struggle, pulling and tugging my body left and right. Q had my hands pinned down, squeezing my wrists so hard, my skin felt like it was ripping off as I squirmed. He tried to kiss me again, moving from my check to my neck.

Get up! GET UP!

I continued to struggle, trying to force him off of me by rapidly turning my body. One last hard twist, almost off the bed, turning my head to the right as I tried to maneuver my leg off the side of the bed.

Eyes tightly closed I tried to gather all of my strength!

He is just high. He doesn't mean it! Searching for any reasoning that would minimize the unimaginable trauma I was experiencing.

I pushed a little more, opening my eyes to see if there was something I could reach for, but my heart stopped when I saw a gun on the nightstand. This was really happening. My life was in danger and there was nothing I could do. Any cloudy judgment I may have had before became painstakingly clear, as fear began to settle in.

My body became motionless, no words, no more wiggling. Just the sight of the black steel bringing everything that mattered into focus. The once tough, fearless girl that "Kristina" created, was suddenly paralyzed with fright.

The room became a blur, a cloud of smoke covered me as I tried desperately to focus on one thing in the room. Hiding all emotion in, reminding myself I was not weak, holding an internal debate and praying for this to just be over at the same time.

Fight! You are stronger than this. Don't let him do this!

Are you crazy? Don't move. This is not worth losing your life!

Get up right now, get up!!

Just keep your eyes closed, it will all be over soon!

This is not real, the music was blaring in the other room. I wasn't sure if anyone was still there or not.

Did they even realize you went to the room with him? I started to question all of my steps, taking inventory of who was there and what everyone was doing.

Your screams would fade into the noise, so why even try. I laid there like a mannequin, stiff and lifeless. A single tear crept slowly down my cheek, the only part of me that could escape from this horrendous moment as I lost control of my body.

Get up! You have to get up!

Just don't move, take your mind somewhere else! Don't move!

Don't cry! Don't move!

"We all know what you white girls are good for." He whispered in my ear as he continued to push his body on top of mine, harder and harder.

Don't cry! Don't move! I continued to coach myself, closing my eyes tightly trying to brace myself for whatever was happening that I now had no control over.

My whole life changed in a matter of minutes, although it seemed like a lifetime. When he finished, I got up, pulled my pants up, and asked him to take me home. As we walked up the steps, he yelled, "Mom I will be back soon," like nothing happened. I had no idea his mom was home. The most traumatizing moment of my life was just another day for him.

I felt dead inside. I didn't scream for help. I barely fought; someone so strong and in control, turned completely helpless in a matter in minutes. I just lost everything, all hope of turning back into that loving girl was gone. Not only was "Blue-eyes" locked away but part of her died that day, never to return.

I didn't say a word on the way to my house, I just stared at the clock on the radio while him and his friend rapped along with Bone-Thugs-N-Harmony. It took 22 minutes to get home, the longest ride of my life. When we pulled into the driveway, my mother and one of her friends were standing there talking. It was like everything was in slow motion.

"Make sure you erase my messages," I vaguely heard him say while laughing as I got out of the car.

"Honey, are you okay?" my mother asked.

I no longer had the energy to muster up a fake smile or even a fake response. I walked right past her but she sounded so far away, it was like I was dreaming.

Hurry, tell her! His car isn't even off the block yet. She has time to stop him!

Don't make a scene! This is all your fault; you should have never lied.

I wanted to tell her so badly, but my mouth just would not move. I was in such a daze it was like I was losing track of time while frozen in it. Before I knew it, I was in the shower, with no clue of how I got there. I stood under the steaming hot water like a statue trying to wash away my shame and gather my emotions so I didn't look weak. It did not take long before I fell to my knees sobbing with my face buried in my hands, rocking back and forth until the hot water turned cold.

Scrub harder! Use more soap! You're never going to get clean! Everyone is going to know!

Oh my God, I am never going to be able to wash this pain and disgust away! I am never going to get this part of me back!

What did I let him do to me? How could I let this happen?

I laid on the hard shower floor, ice cold water, body shivering, legs curled up to my chest, tears intertwining with the flow of water, no longer a distinction between the two. I prayed for each memory of this day to wash down the drain, pleading with God to hear my cries, begging for an answer to how I can move on.

The barriers I had worked so hard to put in place to protect me from the world around me, taught me that showing emotion was a sign of weakness. Any sign of weakness opens up an opportunity for you to be hurt. This tragedy showed me that even allowing myself to laugh with others made me vulnerable. A vulnerability that would strip me of all understanding, reasoning, and logic for years to come.

***

"Are you okay, Krissi?" My Spanish teacher asked.

Clearly, she saw a change within me, in spite of my most valiant efforts to maintain my strong demeanor. *If the walls you built to keep you safe couldn't protect you when it mattered, then what is the point in it all.* I wondered.

"Are you okay?" She'd ask day after day until one afternoon she caught me alone in the hallway.

"Are you okay?" she asked again, coming closer to me and placing her hands over mine as a sign of trust. I stood completely still against the lockers in an empty hall, arms folded across by body with my books held tightly against my chest unable to respond.

"It's okay, you can talk to me. I know something happened. You're not the same person anymore. You don't even laugh. Who hurt you? Who raped you?"

I began to cry uncontrollably. I could not fix my mouth to answer her or even say the word rape. My mind was racing with confusion and my emotions could no longer be contained.

How could she have known? Did someone at the house hear us that day? Or was my demeanor that out of character?

If my teacher knows, who else knows? Oh my God, my life is destroyed! My body language must scream that I am helpless. I must look so weak!

I found myself sitting in the principal's office. There was the principal, assistant principal, school counselor, school liaison officer and me. I was startled by the sound of the door swinging open with aggression. My mother quickly walked in crying and wrapped me in her arms. I hung my head in shame and embarrassment, looking to my left and right to see the reaction of everyone in the room. The pressure of everyone's stares was overwhelming. My body felt so heavy and my mind so disoriented.

"I knew something was wrong. Why didn't you tell me?" my mother cried out.

No response, just a silent cry as my tears drenched her shirt. I just wanted to stay in her arms until this nightmare was over.

The weeks that followed were a blur. Drinking wine, wine coolers, and mixed drinks quickly turned into pure liquor. Weed didn't even touch the surface of the pain, and soon became a mixture of pills, cocaine, ecstasy, and acid. Drinking and popping pills seemed to be the only relief, but somehow no matter how drunk or high I was, those same monsters were still under my bed and the demons remained in the closet.

I was broken, so broken that I would hold onto anything that I thought would even set a piece of me free. The alcohol allowed me to escape the pain and put on a cloak that made me look loving, friendly, and in control. In reality, my life was in shambles. Thousands of unrecognizable, damaged little pieces.

All of the hopes and dreams little Blue-eyes had at one time were just memories that seemed like fairy tales. Anything I could ever see myself becoming seemed distant and out of grasp. All the drugs and spirits that would have frightened me just a few short years earlier, now gave me a sense of purpose and control. I could always count on the drugs and alcohol to be there, the only things that seemed to never let me down. It's funny how substances manage to cloud an already distorted brain. In my delusion, I liked the version of me I was starting to see. This version didn't dwell on the past losses, pain, and trauma. The drugs and alcohol allowed me to use those perceived weaknesses as fuel. When I channeled my hurt and rage properly it gave me a sense of power and control that made the nightmare I was living in more manageable.

Fuck everyone! You are stronger than everything that has happened!

I found myself reciting the same phrase over and over again as I looked in the mirror each morning. The reflection looking back at me was much stronger than the person standing in front of the mirror. She looked and sounded like me, but I was lost somewhere deep inside of her. I wanted so badly to be that strong version of myself, but each day was becoming harder and harder to manage.

My mother continued to try and convince me to file an official report against my rapist, but I was hesitant for a number of reasons. One reason being his father was a cop and honestly, I felt like it was my fault. After everything I had been through, there is no way I wanted to play the victim. After all, I was much too strong to be a victim. I had worked way too hard to create this new version of myself to be viewed as weak again.

Why did you put yourself in that situation? Why do you allow people to hurt you? How could you put yourself in the line of fire?

After several days of these uncontrollable thoughts, I finally caved and went to the police station with my mother. I was a nervous wreck the entire drive. Continuously rubbing my hands together, fidgeting with my clothes, and staring out the window in a daze. I did not say one word, I was so scared! As I started to get out of the car, I became lightheaded and felt like I was going to throw up. Quickly sitting back down in the car, I covered my face with my hands and took a big breath.

You got this! Just breathe!

And just like that, my worst fears became my reality! The officer treated me like everything was my fault. I felt like I was being interrogated instead of helped.

"WHY were you drinking? WHY did you lie about where you were going? WHAT drugs were you doing? WHY didn't you tell anyone? WHY didn't you tell the school officer about the gun? WHY didn't you fight or scream?" The officer asked in a very aggressive and accusatory manner.

The questions were being asked so fast, I didn't even have time to think let alone respond! I started to get so angry, it literally felt like my soul was on fire!

Get it together! Just calm down!

"This is why I didn't tell anyone, you are the fucking reason why! These questions are the reason, it is automatically my fault, and he is the victim!" I shouted enraged as I stood up.

"Mom I am ready to go, I don't have anything else to say."

"Kris, wait. Just listen please!" My mom pleaded.

"No mom, I am done!"

I felt even worse when we left because my own mother started to question me, on the way home.

"Why didn't you tell me about the gun? Why did you lie? What else happened that you didn't tell us?"

"None of that really matters mom, just forget it, it was all my fault. Everything was my fault!" I blurted out in frustration.

"I didn't say that. Why won't you listen, just talk to me!"

"I am listening, and all I hear is everything I did wrong. This is my fault. I created this nightmare and now I have to live with it!"

I never went back to the police station. No official charges were pressed, and everyone at school went on with their lives like nothing happened. The only difference was, I was now the white girl that wanted to destroy a black boy's life.

My popularity faded quickly, and the whispers returned.

"You don't belong here."

"Don't bump into her. She will accuse you of rape."

"I told you she wasn't different from any other white person."

After roughly a week of acting like none of this bothered me, I just stopped going to school and work altogether.

***

Riiinnng!! Riiing!

I don't know why, but there was something harrowing about the sound of a ringing phone. I knew who it was. The police instructed me to go to the doctor to have a rape kit completed and the doctor was due to call with the results any day.

"Hello?" I said, answering the phone.

"Hello, this is Nurse Johnson from Dr. Branson's office. May I speak with Kristina?"

"Yes. This is Kristina." My heart was beating out of my chest.

God please don't let me be pregnant, please don't let me be pregnant.

"Kristina, I have your test results. Would you like your parents to be involved in the conversation?"

"Yes. That's fine." I said reluctantly.

"Unfortunately, we did find that you have three sexually transmitted diseases (STD)," She went on to explain which infections I had and stressed the importance of getting treated quickly as the STDs had been left untreated for several weeks. She explained the medication regimen and how if left untreated properly, STD's would result in my inability to have children in the future. I felt like I was in a movie, an Academy award winning drama.

This can't be true! This can't be happening to me.

The pressure literally made it impossible to breathe. I gasped for air, grabbing my chest and dropping the phone. *My life is over. I cannot be a mom, I even failed at being a woman. It doesn't matter, no one will want me now anyway. Oh God, please just take me now!*

Nothing mattered anymore, my life was over. I was even treated differently at home. My dad wouldn't let my younger siblings come outside with me because he was fearful the person that raped me was going to retaliate. Funny, no one ever stopped me from going outside. I guess it didn't matter if gang members tried to kill me, as long as my siblings weren't in the crossfire.

Once again, the people I felt were charged with protecting me were letting me down. The fact that I was all I had to depend on was becoming crystal clear with each passing day! Within a matter of months, I had completely lost every sense of innocence. Whatever childlike essence that remained in me, was destroyed when I was raped. Pills and laced joints turned into cocaine, and cocaine was mixed with ecstasy. The harder the drug the better chance I had for escape. Mixed drinks were a thing of the past. I was now filling a thermos with pure Absolut Vodka, drinking it like it was water. My soul was full of anger and fire. I finally cracked.

I tried everything to rid my mind of negative thoughts, and nothing was working. Drugs, alcohol, rage, pretending, defending, none of it was enough. One of my close friends, someone I considered family, was at my parent's house with me one night. She tried her best to take my mind off of everything.

"Come on Kris, do you want to watch a movie?" She asked.

"No, I am just going to try and sleep. Give me a Xanax please!"

"Girl! You can't take that shit you have been drinking way too much!"

"I wasn't asking Ashley! Give me my damn pills." I demanded.

"I am just trying to help."

"Then help me sleep!"

I grabbed my pill bottle and tossed two Xanax in my mouth. Washing it down with vodka. I tossed and turned for what seemed like hours.

"I need answers now!" I said as I lunged myself off the couch and headed up the stairs.

"Wait! Wait, where are you going?" My friend asked bewildered.

I raced through the house to my parents' bedroom on the second floor looking through all of my dad's drawers until I finally found his handgun.

"Are you crazy? Put that back right now. Your dad is going to kill you!" She protested.

"Don't call me crazy! I am not crazy! I want, need, and deserve answers! If my dad isn't going to go ask for them and the police are not going to demand them, I will get them myself!"

"Please stop! Listen to yourself." She cautioned.

"Don't stand in my way! I am tired of waiting. I am tired of this being my fault! You do not know how I feel, so until you do get the hell out of my way!"

I took my dad's handgun and went to my rapist's father's house. It felt like an 86 chevy was revving inside my chest. But I just kept walking.

Go home! Stop and think about this! Think about what your father would want you to do!

Just get it over with! You will feel so much better once you have answers or he feels the pain you feel!

Q's father's house was just a few blocks away from our home, so it did not take me long to get there. It was time to get answers, and I wasn't leaving without them. I couldn't look in the mirror another day without knowing why this happened to me.

What did I do to give him the wrong signals? Did he plan it? Is this what he always thought of me? Is this what my so-called friends really think about me? Is this really what they think about all white girls? What did they mean all these years when they said I was different from other white people? What the hell changed?

Ashley tried to talk me out of it all the way to his house,

"Please listen to me, you can't take this back once it's done!" She urged.

"I know!"

As I approached his door, my dad pulled up screaming,

"Baby come here, this is not what you want, trust daddy!" He said, as he motioned for me to come here.

This bitch must have told him where I was going, I looked at Ashley with fire in my eyes.

It didn't matter at this point. Q's father heard the commotion and opened the door and walked outside, quickly closing the door behind him. Our dads knew each other, they were talking back and forth while my mind just spun faster and faster out of control. I didn't hear a word they said, my mind was blank, and I was on a mission. It was like the world around me was still and someone else was in control of my body.

As my friend pleaded with me to go home, my body suddenly went limp as I fell to my knees crying, demanding answers, screaming, "only one of us is walking away from this house tonight!"

"Kris, please get in the car!" my dad begged.

Followed by Q's dad saying, "you have too much to offer, don't do this"

I was completely empty and lifeless at that moment. I could hear their voices but felt as if I was all alone. Still on the ground, bent over with my face between my knees I suddenly felt my dad pick me up and carry me to the car.

"Let's keep this between us! No one needs to know what happened here tonight, it will only make matters worse." Q's dad said to mine as he laid me in the backseat.

The sound of my cries could be heard over the radio all the way home, as Ashley held me in her arms. When we got home, the three of us just sat in the car for what seemed like eternity. No one moved until I was ready to go in the house. As I got out of the car my dad said,

"Your mother is to never hear of this. She wouldn't be able to handle it!"

I didn't even respond. I just walked towards the house as everything around me seemed motionless.

"I love you" my dad's voice echoed down the stairs as I reached the bottom of the steps. I grabbed a bottle of vodka from the back storage room where I kept everything hidden. The night was filled with the sound of my cries as I laid on the couch and drank. I laid lifeless, too emotionally drained to wipe the tears from my eyes, I heard the basement door slowly open.

"Sissy everything is going to be okay." My little brother said, as he kneeled in front of me and wiped the tears from my cheeks."

"I can stay down here with you tonight if you want." He said with his best attempt to comfort me.

"I am okay buddy, it is my job to protect you, remember?" I said with a smirk. "How did you get so brave?"

"You taught me silly" He responded with a big smile as he walked up the stairs.

Tormenting thoughts continued to flood my mind.

They are right. You are only good for partying!

This is all your fault. You put yourself in this situation. You asked for this to happen!

I poured another drink and popped a few more Xanax. Pacing the floor as my mind spun out of control wanting it all to stop.

"Kris, what can I do?" Ashley asked.

"You could have let me talk to him or kill him!" I said, stopping to look at her so she knew I was serious.

"That is not what you really wanted!"

Truly all I wanted to do was call Bee, but there was just too much damage there. I couldn't possibly call after all of this.

He won't listen. You were so mean last time you talked! He will probably think this is all your fault like everyone else!

I sat back on the couch, slumping my body over on Ashley's lap. As tears rolled down my face, she gently rubbed my hair. As the empty bottle fell from my limp hand, the voices instantly became quiet. I don't know if it was all the pills and alcohol I consumed that was finally kicking in. But whatever reason my thoughts came to a halt, I was thankful.

From Bad to Worse

The next few months seemed to go by rather quickly. While I slept through the day and cried through the night, my mother was busy talking to the board of education and got approval to send me to a school in another district.

Maybe this will be a good thing. I don't know anyone. Unfortunately, not knowing people and being trotted off to a new school didn't erase everything that took place a few short months before.

I reluctantly pushed through the first few days. This school was so different, so diverse. For the most part, everyone was welcoming, but I had made up my mind that no one was going to get close enough to hurt me again. After about a month, I started to talk to people a little more and even made a few friends. I thought being around a more diverse crowd might be good for me, but this crowd was diverse in every sense of the word.

The majority of the kids at my new school all came from wealthier families, which meant more money, their own cars, and access to more drugs. It did not take long before I was back into my partying ways, pretending to be okay. As I opened up a little bit, the parties welcomed me with open arms, including all the drugs, alcohol and boys. I started to get close to one particular boy, Anthony. He was so funny and one of the popular kids. He was my get-in-free card to all the parties and my all-access pass to party favors.

While I was trying to bury my pain and shame as deep as possible, Stewy was getting sicker and sicker. My parents brought him home to live with us, nurses came in throughout the week to help, and we had the living room set up like his hospital room. My mother started working to help balance some of her emotional strain and my dad took some family medical leave to care for my brother. Going home was harder than ever before, looking at my brother I was fearful I was looking at myself and still had no one to turn to.

Stay strong, don't let him see that you're scared!

I wonder if he is in pain! God, just take me instead. I have fucked up everything here anyway. He deserves a chance to be happy and healthy!

As I was trying to hold it together, my dad was morphing right before my eyes. Although he wasn't our biological father, he raised us. Watching one of his oldest children die, with absolutely nothing he could do to stop it was too much for him to handle. Soon the street drugs were not enough to suppress his pain and he started using my brother's prescription medication to numb his emotions. The man that I once longed to spend time with, was still there physically but emotionally and mentally he was gone, and I couldn't blame him.

"Dad, are you okay?" I would ask as he sat next to my brother's hospital bed like a zombie.

"Dad?"

"Yeah, what's wrong?"

"Nothing, I was checking on you. Are you okay?" I asked.

"Yeah, honey I am fine!"

I wish I could make all this pain go away! Life is so unfair!

While dad was turning into a shell of himself, I was still being overlooked or picked on depending on the day. It seemed like no matter what I did, it wasn't good enough for my mother. I spent too much time with friends, too much time on the phone, not enough time with Stewy. I was always too distracted in her eyes. In the midst of her pain and the thought of losing her son, she never stopped to think she was pushing her daughter even further away or maybe my many distractions were the only way to cope. No one had considered the trauma I was experiencing watching my brother fade away. Looking at him, for me, was me staring death in the face! On top of all the other reasons I had for not wanting to be home, the fear of becoming sick and seeing my fate unfold in front of me was simply too much.

How long will it be before I start getting sick? Is it going to hurt? I am scared! Girl, get out of your head and live in the moment before it is too late!

I just could not understand how they, as adults, couldn't cope with the pain and pressures in their daily lives, but ignored how their teenage daughter was falling apart. Emotions and actions all screaming for help and love, all left unanswered!

I am never going to be good enough for her.

Mom probably wishes it was me laying in that bed and not him!

Why in the hell does she hate me so much?

***

"What are you doing?" I woke up startled with the weight of his body on mine. He grabbed my hands and pulled them toward his chest.

"What are you doing?" I asked again, in a panic.

"Play with my nipples"

"What? Why?" I asked hesitatingly.

"Because I like it." He said.

My cry became so painful I struggled for air, and finally let out a cry so emotionally intense my whole body shook in fear.

"Daddy, Stop!"

This was a fear beyond description. The man I loved more than life itself; the man I trusted, and I believed would lay down his life to protect me was sexually assaulting me. I felt trapped and the trauma from Q came flooding back with vengeance.

"Get off of me!" I cried, looking into a dark, empty hull of the man I call Dad. Who was this man? It couldn't be my dad. I stared at a man with an empty soul, a complete stranger was staring back at me. His voice was even different.

There was a shift of energy in the room as the intensity of my cry magnified. This was the first time I can say I truly felt God's presence. It was evident that God heard my cries. Dad began wailing uncontrollably. It's as if he was fighting to regain control of himself. He jumped off of the couch crying and begging for my forgiveness.

"I'm so sorry! What was I about to do? Please, forgive me; please stop crying, please don't wake your mom up!" He pleaded in desperation.

I heard his apologies as a distant whisper in my head, as the room around me seemed void of life.

I have been right all along! I have no one in this world! I should have fought back. I should have forced him to pull the trigger! I am worth nothing but my body, an empty tomb. Completely soulless and powerless. I have nothing to give! The thoughts flashed through my mind solidifying my sense of defeat and worthlessness.

I was officially broken into too many pieces to put back together. Just remnants of what could have been. Dad ran out of the room, and I sat on the corner of the couch, curled in a ball, hugging my knees for dear life, spiraling deeper and deeper into depression and thoughts of self-harm.

I am so worthless and only good for one thing. I have no purpose left. Why am I here? Am I that unlovable?

The next day, I forced a fake grin on my face and headed off to school. I moved through each class as normal as possible for several days to come. Roughly a week passed before I decided to tell my mother, but for some reason I didn't have the strength to tell her face to face.

I have to tell her! Oh my god, this is going to be a nightmare. Why am I wasting my breath? She is going to blame me anyway!

I couldn't get the thought of being looked at with shame or embarrassment out of my head. I certainly could not run the risk of being interrogated again! All of the thoughts and memories from that night went into a four-page letter that I left on the kitchen table on my way to school that day. I went to stay at a friend's house for a few days so I wouldn't have to face anyone right away.

When my mother finally called to tell me she got the letter, we sat in what felt like eternal silence.

"Hello," I said, nervously.

"Are you okay?" Mom asked.

"I am fine."

"When are you coming home?"

When am I coming home? Is that the only question she has? Not sorry! Not, I love you but "when are you coming home?" I remained silent for a few moments trying desperately to gather my thoughts.

"Kris, are you still there?" Mom asked.

"Yeah, I am here."

I was physically holding the phone, but my thoughts had already shifted into defense mode. All I wanted was for my mother to love me and defend me. To choose me over everything else! But she couldn't. I was left with the impossible task of another adult decision that could change the course of my entire family's life.

"Do you want me to make him leave?" She asked with reservation.

I remained silent for a few moments before asking, "Did you talk to him?"

"Yes, do you want me to make him leave?" She repeated.

"What did he say?"

"He said he didn't remember that night and he would never do anything to hurt you."

He answered as I suspected and truly wanted to believe. I wanted so deeply to believe that this was all a dream, that my family did love me, and would never hurt me. But how could that possibly be true when all I felt was pain or invisible when I was around them. Mom, cowardly, put the responsibility back on me. It was a catch 22: push my pain and trauma aside to keep my family together or tell her to put my daddy out on the streets. I was being given an underhanded ultimatum.

How is this fair? How do I choose?

It never dawned on me that my mother may have been crying out for help herself. That maybe she was just as hurt and confused as I was. Perhaps she secretly needed me to be her strength and make a decision that would force her to ask him to leave. It is hard to imagine but very possible that during these times, we both felt invisible and out of control.

All I ever wanted was to feel whole and have my father. I never imagined at 17- years old I would want to end it all. I felt no purpose, no passion, no drive, no reason. Just complete deadness inside! Everywhere I turned there was pain. Every road I tried to go down was empty.

In a world that was supposed to be so big and full of promise, I was all alone. All purposeful desires gone, nothing but dirt and debris left in the wake of a chaotic storm!

Beautiful Disaster

"Where are you going now? You are never home!" Mom interrogated.

"I am going to work and a then over to a friend's house."

"What friends? I never know what you are doing. You need to spend more time with your brother!"

"Why would I want to be here when you are always picking on me? I will see you tonight!"

Things were so different at home, I always felt trapped and tormented by my pain. Everyone seemed to get quiet when I was around, making me feel like a stranger in my own home. Actions and stares from my family made me feel punished for everything that happened as if it was my fault. I started to avoid eye contact with my parents, spending as much time as possible in my room or away from home all together.

What did I do to deserve this? I just want to crawl into a hole and disappear! I am sure they wouldn't even notice I was gone!

Searching for acceptance and companionship anywhere I could find it, I forced myself to get closer to some of my classmates. They had asked me to hangout several times, out of fear and suspicion I continued to avoid letting people in! However, the amplifying tension between my parents and me made me feel deflated. Opening up to my new friends helped bring some sense of significance to my pitiful existence.

Soon Anthony and I became more than just friends. It felt good to trust someone again. I slowly opened up about bits and pieces of my trauma but wasn't ready to share all of my secrets. Fearful that he would look at me differently, I remained guarded with "Kristina" manning the ship. Still, we became closer, and I started to share more. My desire to be loved continued to distort my discernment and exploit my weaknesses. "Kristina" tried desperately to chain my heart with lock and key, while my mind was persistent on painting pictures of a happily ever after that would never come true!

All my efforts to come out of my shell continued to fail in my mother's eyes. Although she made no endeavor to know any of my new friends and failed to pay attention to the daily changes bursting out through my actions and appearance. She still exhausted all of her energy to identify something wrong with each aspect of my life. I was amazed that she was so clueless about all the drugs and drinking but thought she was so knowledgeable when it came to my new companions.

"Mom, give me a reason why you don't like Anthony?"

"He just uses you" she blurted out flippantly.

"Uses me for what? I asked. You don't know anything about our relationship outside of him being a boy and me being your daughter."

"You would lie for him anyway," She insisted. "You probably give him all your money."

"Think what you want to. All I know is he was there for me when you should have been and weren't" I knew that would hurt.

Just more shallow and unvetted responses. Consumed with my bitterness, it never occurred to me that maybe she really was trying to protect me. What I saw as her wanting to control me could have truly been her fear of something else tragic happening to me.

I struggled to see why she thought he was trying to use me. More importantly, why I was clearly still invisible unless she felt like attacking me. Could she really be this blind, or is my trauma being pushed under the rug like her crumbling relationship with Dad?

There is no way she doesn't know about the drugs! It was almost like I wanted to get caught, because at least then I would know she was paying attention.

Life has a relentless way of taking us back in time, re-playing events over and over, wishing we could change the course of our actions or the outcomes that were a re-sult of those actions. Unfortunately, in life there is no reset button. We make the choices we make and regardless of if they turn out to be the best long-term decisions or not, we are left to live with our choices, the consequences that follow them, and the lingering feelings that haunt our minds.

*****

As the fights between Mom and I intensified from small windstorms to full tornadoes, I couldn't stand to be in the same room as her anymore. If we were not fighting, I was making a conscious effort to not even look in her direction. My rage and resentment towards her grew daily, continued thoughts and disbelief that she didn't protect me. How could she pick a man over her own flesh and blood? How could she not love me enough to see I was dying inside and all I wanted was my mom? Maybe I had gotten so good at hiding, that even she couldn't see my pain.

I soon made the decision to move out. I wasn't going to sit around while someone who didn't protect me tried to control me! With each passing thought my anger towards her grew. How was it okay for me to date someone in their 20's and skip school, but she distrusted Anthony who was my age?

Every day I found myself asking another question, trying to reason with how a mother could push her daughter away, ignore the pain that was turning her into someone else, and make her feel like she deserved it all. Nothing made sense! How could my actions be questioned when it is acceptable for my body to be abused, my mind crushed, and my self-identity stripped from me?

Typical Mom! Let's ignore how you are used and treated. Just put all the focus on your daughter and brush your ridiculous excuse for a life off to the side!

My anger boiled out of control with questions that would never be asked or answered,

"Why do you find it necessary to try to protect me now? Where was all of this motherly love when I needed you the most? When I needed you stand up for me, when even the police didn't have my back."

These feelings made it impossible to claim my spirit and ask these questions. Questions that may have bridged some gaps and allowed room for healing. My tainted heart would not allow me to see past the damage already done. In my eyes, I started to lose my mom before my father died, and once he was gone, I lost everything. I was an orphan, unwanted, unloved, and unseen.

My spiral out of control continued to get worse within days of moving out. I started to miss more school, consuming the majority of my time with work. Working more meant more money, which meant more partying, which meant less time at the house. As soon as I turned 18-years old, I dropped out of school, moved in with a long-lost cousin, and eventually got a place with my close friend, Penelope, who I met a few years earlier. I had no real guidance in life, just me moving through the day-to-day functions, which for me, was working, paying bills, and partying.

Dropping out of school allowed me to be more flexible with working hours and the type of jobs I applied for. Soon I started working second shift at a local factory, quickly buddying up with much older co-workers.

In a wild turn of events, the closeness between Anthony and I turned into manipulation. He used my desire to have a trusting relationship with someone as his opportunity to make me believe he was the only one that cared. He hated the new friendships I was making and used every opportunity to make me feel like I was doing something wrong by trying to find some peace and happiness. Every argument grew with hatred.

"You are hanging out after work again." Anthony asked with irritation in his voice.

"Yes, is that a problem?"

"You don't even know these people. You are such a fool. When are you going to stop thinking everyone is your friend?"

"What are you talking about?" I snapped back. "You don't know them. You are always hanging out! Kind of like the pot calling the kettle black here, isn't it? Or did you suddenly forget all the phone calls I get about your nights at the club?"

"Whatever! You will learn. You cannot count on them,and I am not Bee."

"You sure the hell ain't! He would never say anything to hurt me!"

"Maybe you should run back to him? Oh wait, you were never his girlfriend, I forgot."

"Funny, you are right. I am a fool. A fool to think that I could share anything with you, and you would not act like a little boy when you didn't get your way."

"Listen to yourself, you are being crazy. You know I love you; I am the only one that loves you. I put you first, your parents are not even there for you."

"And on that note, I am gone, have a good night sir!"

"What!! Wait!! Listen to me, where are you going? Why can't you talk now?"

"Don't worry about it, maybe I will call Bee! You should be careful what you wish for! I am no longer the girl I told you stories about. You should think about that next time you open your mouth."

"Krissi"

"Goodnight!"

The realization that I wasn't good enough unless his needs came first, hit like a ton of bricks. I immediately started looking inward, trying to see what I did wrong, how I misread the relationship. Searching my heart for answers. Part of me wanted to make it work, the other part of me knew I just did not want to be wrong about letting someone in my life again.

I was only pretty enough until the next girl came by. I was only worth spending time with if I was making him look good or having sex with him. I was a master at making him look good! Showing up early to every basketball game and dressed to kill. I showed up at every practice and cheered him on, even if his side pieces were also in the stands. I was the definition of a perfect girlfriend and losing more of my dignity in the process! Giving him everything I so desperately wanted from someone else! I would sit in the stands next to his mother. Laughing while I pretended, I didn't notice the other girls. I was falling apart inside as I blamed myself for the way I was being treated.

You destroyed another friendship by crossing lines. You created this storm! You had the opportunity to have a real friendship and messed everything up with your silly emotions.

Anthony and I were friends from the moment we met, just as Bee and I started. He was so nice and seemed to be caring, always making me laugh, introducing me to people, and showing me around. The person he became as a boyfriend, was someone completely different! A new school, yes, but I was still followed by these dark clouds! The storm just seemed to shift in whatever direction I was moving in. I went from being bullied or looked at as the mean girl in some cases, to being laughed at because I looked like a fool trusting him. Calling him my boyfriend when he cheated with every new girl that came to the school. In the same breath, he used every opportunity to make me feel like I was doing something wrong.

Why the hell is love so important anyway? You are so much happier alone! You don't need anyone, certainly not a boy!

I was crushed, but yet continued to go back to Anthony when I knew he was taking advantage of my pain. When we were together there was nothing but pain, arguments, and us fighting because someone was calling him while I was with him. I felt like I was repeating my mother's cycle with my dad. The only difference was, they didn't always seem broken. Maybe this is what my mom was trying to shield me from, perhaps she could see the storm before it started!

Here goes this damn phone ringing again! Yep, let's ignore it like we don't hear it!

"Really?" I yelled.

"What?"

"So, you didn't hear your phone ringing? Or, you just don't want to answer because I am here?"

"Don't start that shit."

"Sounds good! I will talk to you later!" I said as I stood up to leave.

"Stop leaving every time you get mad!"

"Oh, you are confused! I am not mad. This is me being tired!"

Still, I continued to answer when he called. It was like I was drawn to the fighting. Fighting had become such a normal part of my life; it was almost like a security blanket in some way. It reminded me that I still had feelings under all the pain.

However, you can only rely on limitations and make-believe boundaries for so long. Before I knew it, all that anger quickly turned to violence!

***

As I approached his door, I heard a girl's voice laughing in the background. My body immediately tensed up as I knocked on the door. Slowly looking to the right of me where Penelope anxiously stood. Shaking my head back and forth with anticipation of what explanation he was going to feed me today. To my surprise, one of my so-called friends was sitting on the couch.

You have got to be fucking kidding me!

"Hi bae!" He said with a crack in his voice as he opened this door.

Pushing him out of my way, I nonchalantly walked into the living room.

"Hey! What are you doing here?" I asked with no expectation of receiving an acceptable response.

"Hey girl! Just hanging out."

"Do you often hang out half dressed?" I said with a raised eyebrow and a shrug of the shoulders.

It is amazing how much strength you have when you have been hurt and betrayed. The disrespect was so unreal, he didn't even try to hide it. It was obvious from the make-shift bed of sheets on the living room floor that they were just intimate. That and the fact that he wasn't fully dressed. I had seen everything I needed to see, without hesitation I threw her things off the balcony as I let out a desperate cry.

"How could you do this to me again? Out of all the people in the world, you had to pick someone I know!"

My rant continued to pour out of my mouth while I tossed more and more things off of the balcony.

"Krissi, wait it is not what you think!" She cried out.

"Shut the fuck up. I am not talking to you!"

"Krissi, I am sorry! I promise nothing happened!" She pleaded again.

Before I knew it, my hands were around her throat pushing her to the balcony as he grabbed me from behind!

"Let her GO!" He screamed.

"Krissi, please stop!" Penelope shouted as she tried pulling my hands from around her neck.

"Why are you protecting her and shitting on me? What did I do to deserve this?" My screams continued to get louder. "Why do you continue to take advantage of my insecurities, my needs, my unconditional LOVE? I gave you all of me! Shared things with you no one knows, and you just stomped on it!"

"Just listen to me!" He demanded.

I was once again, faced with the lingering question, *Am I that unlovable?*

As he pulled me through the living room and kitchen, I grabbed a pan and threw it across the room hitting her in the head. Then I quickly grabbed another pan trying to transfer my emotional pain onto him physically.

We wrestled back and forth, bumping into every counter and wall, knocking things off the kitchen table, and breaking dishes with all my misdirected anger. The kitchen looked like a group of toddlers just had a food fight. Things were everywhere.

"Krissi, please come on! He is not worth this shit!" Penelope begged as she pulled my arm trying to drag me towards the door.

"This is not over! I promise you will feel what I feel some day. I don't care what it takes! The pain, the embarrassment, the anger, the rage knowing you have been betrayed. You are going to feel every last bit of what you did to me!"

Pulling out of the apartment complex, I was once again vowing to myself to never let anyone in, never trust, never love!

As I stared in the mirror that night, I asked myself, *how could you be so stupid? How did you not see what was right in front of you? Was mom right this whole time?*

Within the next few days, he was back on bended knee begging me to forgive him; promising it would never happen again. He even called girls in front of me and told them to never call him again. It was only a month before my world spun out of control again, finding out he was sleeping with one of our old co-workers.

What the fuck is wrong with me? He is never going to change!

I was turning into my mother. As long as the morning came with an apology, there I was brushing everything under the rug. The thing is… my pain ran deep into my core and "Kristina" was not willing to allow the rug to cover it all. Each day another brick was piled on top of my walls, another layer of armor added to protect me. Vengeance was real and my aggrieved mind was forming a strategic plan of attack. I was no longer in love. I was so methodical and tactful with my plan for revenge that I was beginning to scare myself.

***

Trying to take my mind off of all the drama I decided to hang out with some friends. On our way out, we stopped at McDonalds to see some old coworkers and a friend, Amber. I didn't work there anymore but I often would swing by to say hi.

Amber was sharing all the details of rumors she heard about Anthony and his new lover Melissa. I stood stoic, putting on my most unfazed face, but inside, I was an inferno of rage. The voice ordering from the intercom crackled in: "Yes, I'd like a number two with cheese and a coke"

The voice was familiar. Amber and I looked at each other with surprise.

Couldn't be...

It was! Melissa, Anthony's new lover, was pulling up.

"What's up girl? What are you doing up here?" Melissa asked with a surprised look. Maybe it was her guilty conscience, or it could have been due to the fact that I was standing in the drive-thru window, clearly out of place, in regular, non-McDonalds work attire.

"Oh, just hearing all about your love affair with Anthony!" I said with a mischievous smile.

"What are you talking about?" Melissa asked.

"You tell me! We can do this the easy way where no one gets hurt or, you can continue to lie to me and I beat the shit out of you for being so fucking disgraceful! Choice is yours!"

"It is not like that! He said you two were not together anymore. It was just one night, I swear!"

In an instant, a strength I have never known came over me. I jumped out the drive through window and pulled her through the car window and drug her to the ground. Every swing of my fist released another painful affair, another lie, another level of deceit. There was no turning back. I was no longer in control of my body. The sounds of the vehicles and people passing by went unheard. It was as if I was levitating above my body, watching everything play out with no say so about what my next move was going to be.

I found myself standing over her, as she lay on her side, blood-soaked shirt, bruised and swollen face, ripped clothing, and my racing heart matching the rhythm of the police siren getting closer and closer.

The storm brewing inside was beyond my control at this point. So much agony at the thought of not being loved, continuously being overlooked, being taken for granted, and not being ENOUGH!! My longing desire to be loved overshadowed my ability to see what was right in front of me for so long. When I finally did, a whirlwind of storms collided together producing something so magnificent, so catastrophic, and simply unstoppable. There was no turning back now! "Kristina" stacked the walls stories high, guards at every turn, piercing stares that sucked the life out of my enemies. My fury pushed me through the days to follow, I was becoming a living nightmare disguised as an innocent beauty.

Game on!

I would have done anything to make him feel my pain even if it meant I was hurting myself in the process!

Let's hit him where it hurts the most! You have to hurt his ego and pride, that is the only way!

The manipulated was now the manipulator, the "Kristina" that middle school created had been reborn stronger with a wrath I didn't think was humanly possible! The monsters that hid under my bed for so long and the demons in my closet, were now out to play. All the built-up pain and anger in my 110lb petite frame was enough to bring the Empire State Building down.

Bottled up rage, frustration, humiliation, and bitterness can turn the purest soul dark and vengeful. This mixture of emotion gave life to a beautiful disaster.

I will happily stand in the middle of the tumbling bricks surrounded by dust just to watch him crawl away!

Damaged Beyond Repair

I quickly transitioned into a mistress of manipulation. It became so effortless, one word, one glance, and I could persuade these simple boys to do whatever I wanted.

Anger transformed to laughter; seductive eye contact turned vindictive. When new affairs were brought to my attention, I laughed in his face and went out of my way to make sure he saw pictures of me with other guys he knew. There were no more tears to cry, only hatred brewing deep in my soul. The promise I made to ensure he felt every part of my pain, was coming to fruition. I made sure of it.

"Kristina" attended every party, front and center, controlling the room from the moment she walked in, seductively walking past each potential boy toy sizing all of them up in one head-to-toe glance. Raise my eyebrow, a slight lift of the shoulder, smiling just enough for my dimples to appear before gliding through the crowd with small glances back, making sure I kept their attention.

In an effort to get even, I intentionally placed myself where he would be. Pulling power from the looks of disgust on his face while he was forced to watch another man dance with me. Each small turn around the living room floor of the house party, I slid closer to my dance partner, Eric. Slowly touching his hand, adjusting the positioning from my ribcage to my hip. Tossing my hair, glancing over my shoulder, making eye contact with Anthony while my dance mate pulled me close. Chest to chest, allowing the slow melodies to take me to a place of ecstasy, knowing Anthony couldn't help but watch.

My body felt exhilarated! The relaxing sounds of slow jams, the sensual feeling of passion and desire, dim lighting, and the tantalizing scent of Eric's cologne made me eventually forget that Anthony was in the room.

"May I cut in?" I heard Anthony request.

"Actually, we were just leaving, right?" I answered with a smug look on my face.

"Yes ma'am, we are!" Eric responded as he reached out his hand, guiding me towards the door.

That evening I felt victorious, gloating in the pain I saw in Anthony's eyes. Waking up next to someone else allowed me to feel empowered, but the feeling withered rather fast. I didn't want any of these new boy toys to be a permanent fixture in my life, they were all just pawns. A way to shift the playing field. I had no desire to level or balance the indiscretions, the goal was to shift all the power in my direction regardless of cost. So blind with hatred and a hunger for revenge, I could not realize the self-harm being done. My actions were belittling, not only to him but to myself as well.

I stooped to his levels of disrespect and inconsideration. So determined to be in control of myself and my surroundings, I never stopped to examine the fact that I was hurting myself more. The non-stop drinking, drugs, and putting myself in situations where I could not control the room was only placing me in the path of danger and self-destruction. But I didn't care; I felt alive, free, and powerful.

The walls I started to build so long ago were finally complete. Constructed with bricks of indescribable pain, and the cement of unbelievable rage that you only read about in horror stories. Walls built with the highest quality craftsmanship, indestructible. My eyes told the story of a girl lost in her despair. I was no longer willing to fight fair!

As humans, we find it hard to imagine a loveless life. A life with no true companionship. The thought of having no one to share secrets with is unheard of. Most people would find this sad and unmanageable. For me, it was reality. Sadly, I was becoming more comfortable with sexual pleasure than companionship. My broken spirit allowed me to portray myself as emotionless, uncommitted, and self-pleasing.

Anthony continued to try and push his way into my life, but my security system on my newly constructed walls was "bullshit proof". I found myself purposely hurting him every chance I got, like pulling the strings on a puppet. All attempts to connect with me emotionally, failed horribly. I had nothing left to give and nothing left for him to take.

"Bae, why are you so cold? You won't even hold a conversation with me anymore." Anthony asked with growing suspicion.

"You sound like a broken record. I don't have anything to talk about."

"If we are going to make this work, you have to meet me halfway," he tried to reason.

"I am sorry! When did I tell you I wanted to make this work? That ship sailed about four girls ago."

"Don't do that! Don't push me away."

"I learned from the best and I am growing tired of this repeat conversation. My tears are all dried up, my love."

"See, even when I am doing right you find something wrong. Cool off and call me later."

"Don't hold your breath." I responded in laughter as I hung up the phone and poured another drink. "Stupid, stupid boy!" I chanted as I prepared another line of cocaine.

Work, home, party, rest, repeat. I found myself talking to my family less and staying secluded in my bubble. For a brief moment, I thought I was starting to find my happy place. No one to answer to, only good times, laughter, and booty calls.

Just as I thought I was in control, like the subtle winds at the start of a tornado, this was only a calm before the storm.

***

Stewy started to get increasingly sick and was soon hospitalized. Each time I went to see him, my heart ached more with uncontrollable thoughts of the days to come. My mom just didn't understand, all she could see is I wasn't there every second of the day.

"You are never with your brother! You act like your friends are more important."

"Okay, Mom."

"You need to stop putting yourself first and think about your family," she said.

"That is laughable! All I do is think about my family."

The dialogue between her and I should have been on repeat. It seemed like every time we talked, I was being criticized, resulting in me becoming even more distant. There was no sense in arguing with her around Stewy. He needed a peace in his last few days. I couldn't stand the thought of his final memory of me being in an argument in his hospital room about pointless shit.

Maybe if it was me in that bed instead of him, she would finally care about me! Fuck it, I don't do anything right anyway. My brother knows how much I love him. I wish like hell I could trade places with him. I would do it in a heartbeat!

***

Ring...Ring...

My heart dropped at the sound of the phone ringing. The feeling in the pit of my stomach convinced me this call was the one that had kept me up for many nights, tossing and turning with the dreaded thought of saying goodbye for the last time...

"Hello" I answered, trying not to express the nervousness rushing through my veins.

"Kris, you need to get to the hospital now..." An extended pause was all the confirmation I needed. It was time.

"Kris, if you want to say goodbye, please go to the hospital now." My mother forced out with a crack in her voice. "I just left the hospital for a few minutes; Tiffany is with him now and I am headed back that way."

"Okay, I am on my way." I responded.

I glanced around the living room trying to gather my thoughts before jumping in the car. I stood still just for a moment, hands palms down on the kitchen table as I evaluated my life wrapped up in a little bow on this wooden round tabletop. A deck of cards, several bottles of liquor, weed, and cocaine...

It should be me in that hospital bed! I am just throwing my life away while he continued to fight for his!

"What's wrong, Krissi?" Penelope asked. I was home with Penelope and her boyfriend Marco at the time, we were all roommates.

I tried to answer her but all that I could do was stare with my disdain, and heavy, sorrow filled eyes.

"It's Stewy." She softly said as her eyes began to fill with tears. Her expression was pure compassion and sympathy. She did not need to say anything else. I could see all of my pain radiating across the room to her as tears started to fall from both of our eyes.

"Come on! I will drive." Marco said, gently wrapping his arm around my shoulder giving me a squeeze.

The thirty-minute car ride to the hospital seemed to take a lifetime. My thoughts were so scattered, racing with flashbacks of any childhood memory I could conjure up. Pleading with God to allow me the opportunity to say goodbye. I found myself even bargaining with God, as long as I could say goodbye and see his beautiful eyes one more time, I was willing to try anything.

God please! I am begging you. I will never drink again! Please, please just let me say goodbye!

My begging and pleading with God were not enough to stop the racing thoughts from drowning out the sounds of the radio. Covering my face with my hands, elbows resting on my knees and head bent low, I cried. A slow, silent cry for all the faded memories, the pieces of our story I couldn't remember, the chapters of his life he would never get to write, and all the moments we were not going to be able to share!

What should I say to him when I get there? Will he be able to hear me? How long will it be before it is me laying in that bed?

As we pulled in front of the hospital, I remained focused on the brick outlines as my eyes slowly followed the pattern up the towering building. As I went to close the car door, my body froze as I tried to push my emotions down as far as I possibly could before walking in. With each step another memory came to mind.

The hospital was dark and quiet this time of night. Everything seemed eerie as we walked down what seemed to be a never ending hallway. Penelope gently rubbed my back with one hand and held my hand with the other. My legs felt heavier with every step as if weights were being added to my ankles.

My body grew heavy with sorrow as we approached his hospital room. With my head hung low and one hand bracing the door frame, I turned and walked into the doorway. Tiffany looked up and slowly shook her head…

I was too late, he was gone.

My silly, selfish desire to not fight anymore robbed me of the opportunity to say goodbye! This whole time I was trying to prove to myself I was in control by pulling away. Instead, I allowed other peoples' actions, my mother in particular, to get in the way of my happiness once again.

If you would have just told her how you felt, you would have had more time with him!

With my head leaned against the car window, I stared into the dark night wondering if the mysterious unknown mansion in the sky is real. Could Stewy truly be standing beyond all the darkness, watching me journey home? Bloodshot eyes, a swollen face, and an exhausted mind was all I had left. I followed each star as if it were a road map leading me to Stewy's heavenly room.

It seemed to take hours for us to drive home, not one word spoken, the car was so quiet I could hear myself breathing. I continued to gaze out the window while Penelope reached back and held my right hand, reassuring me I was not alone. They were both so supportive, two true friends. They honestly cared about my pain and deeply wanted to help me through it all.

Of course, instead of welcoming the help and love, I did what I do best and found another distraction. The next week was dedicated to Stewy's case manager and I getting all the necessary paperwork in order. Trips to the social security office and secretary of state, oddly enough, helped distract my mind from all the painful emotions.

Holding his birth certificate and death certificate in my hands at the same time was so surreal. We headed back to my house to get the last of the documents needed before meeting with the funeral director. I was so mentally distracted when I walked in, I didn't even notice Anthony sitting in the living room. As I grabbed the manila envelope from the table, I was startled by the sound of his voice coming from behind me. I urgently turned around with aggression, as my eyes met with his; nothing but pure hatred coursing through my veins.

"Hey bae!" He said in a very nonchalant manner.

"My name is Kristina, and what are you doing here?" I asked, heading for the door.

"I just want to be here for you. We can get past all this. Come on bae!"

"You are unbelievable! Everything is not an opportunity for you to creep your way back into my life."

"I know, just let me be here for you. You shouldn't be alone right now."

"I am not alone! You are so delusional to think you are the only person I can call on. I don't need you at all. What I need is for my brother to be standing in front of me healthy and telling me I was a fool for ever trusting you!"

"WOW" He said in shock.

"I am in a rush. Don't be here when I get back and leave my key on the table."

As I closed the van door, I felt a weight being lifted off of my shoulders. I said things to Anthony that morning that I should have been brave enough to say in a calm voice at least a year prior. I just smiled, thinking, *thanks big brother*!

Stewy gave me the strength I needed to stand strong and say goodbye for good. It was like he was standing behind me, backing me up, strengthening my posture and giving me the confidence to focus on what I truly needed in that moment instead of putting what Anthony's ego needed to hear first.

***

"Are you ready?" Stewy's case manager Maria asked as she parked the van.

"As ready as I am going to be!" I responded with a deep sigh.

Slowly walking to the funeral home entrance, I hesitated to grab the handle. Although I felt a little lighter on my feet, this was one step closer to forever.

Just breathe!

My hand started to quiver as I struggled to open the envelope, a rush of emotion started to take over as I reached for his death certificate. Finalizing the paperwork was like the final step in goodbye! This made it all real! No more holidays together, no more birthdays to celebrate, no more hospital visits. His struggle was finally over. I was happy for him but overcome with sadness for Tiffany and me. Standing at the crossroads saying,

"Until we meet again!"

Once again, my mind was filled with questions I would never be able to ask, and a chapter of my life was over without any true closure.

Mom was right, I should have spent more time with him! Did he really know how much I loved him? Could he feel my fear of getting sick when I was around? Was he upset because he was sick and I wasn't?

My parents held three days of viewing before the funeral. Mom's face was full of pain and agony. No words needed to be said, it was clear she didn't want to say goodbye. Dad was physically in the room but mentally in another world, he silently shook the hands of everyone who greeted him. Just emotionless, empty stares as people came in and out of the church.

By the day of the funeral, Stewy's skin was so discolored from bruising, you could see every stroke of the makeup brush. The funeral home and church did an amazing job of keeping everything as clean and nice as possible. However, after three days there are just certain changes in our body that cannot be camouflaged. I knew the final phase of this chapter was approaching its end as the viewing room of the church started to clear out. Within a few short minutes, all that remained in the room was my *only* big brother, Penelope, and me. I sat staring at the casket for just a few moments, becoming lost in time. The sounds of the secondhand clock hanging on the wall became increasingly loud and soon faded out by the piano softly playing in the sanctuary.

"Ma'am are you ready?" One of the funeral home members asked softly.

"Just one more minute please." I whispered.

I sat bent over in my chair, hands on my cheeks, fingers covering my eyes, elbows on my knees, tears slowly rolling down my face landing on the floor in front of me. Penelope rubbed my back, reminding me of the walk to his hospital room that early morning of January 6, 1999. As I took a deep breath and stood up, I glanced at the funeral home team and nodded my head yes to indicate I was ready.

"If you would like to have a seat in the sanctuary, we will be right in to get started."

"I would like to stay and close the casket myself if you don't mind."

"Are you sure? We are happy to help you through this step."

"I am sure. I want to hold his hand until the end. He would do the same for me."

I carefully placed my right hand over his while my left hand touched the top of the casket as I started to push down. I bent down and gently kissed his forehead as I whispered,

"I love you so much! I am incredibly sorry this happened to you! You would have been an amazing man, loving father, and a wonderful husband. Kiss our father for me! I will try to make you both proud, I promise."

Each word spoken was delivered with another tear, slowly rolling down my face, bouncing from my shirt to his collar and tie.

"Until we meet again!" With both hands planted on top of the casket, I leaned back with my head raised to the ceiling. One more deep sigh as I hesitated to lift my hands from the seal on his final resting place.

Arm and arm with Penelope, we walked into the sanctuary. My body felt weightless as I forced myself to tune out all the distractions surrounding me. I sat in the front row of the church as music played and the pastor shared stories of my brother's life. I didn't hear one word. Like our dad, I was physically in the room but mentally I was gone.

By the age of 19, I had to say goodbye forever to two of the most loving and beautiful human beings ever born. One of which I was never blessed with the opportunity to truly know, passing at the age of 36-years old. The other, a life cut way too short! Being diagnosed with an unforgiving disease at 11-years old and ending a good fight at the age of 25. I missed the opportunity for a real loving relationship with my brother because I failed to take advantage of the time by letting life get in the way of what was most important. My big brother was gone, another chapter of my life closing with a less than desirable ending. I sat in silence, not realizing the funeral was ending, until my aunt tapped my back from the seat behind me.

Walking out of the church, going to the cemetery, and the dinner afterwards was unreal. I felt like I was in the Twilight Zone. As I looked around the dining hall of the church the room seemed to be roaring with laughter and stories of Stewy, while I sat still unable to engage at all. My body was limp, no energy for anything or anyone. People continued to bring me drinks and food, all of which was left untouched.

My uncle came behind me giving me the warmest hug possible and kissing me on the cheek. I couldn't respond. Slightly moving my head to the left, I gently brushed my face against his. As the evening reached a close, I went home and slept the night away. I didn't answer the phone for days, barely leaving my room. Finally gathering myself emotionally in the days to come.

You are strong and beautiful, go be great for him! It is time to let go and forgive yourself! It is time for your life to begin!

Time to Let Go

*E*yes fixated on the ceiling; a smile of optimism on my face; and a hopeful stretch to start the day. A new year and a new me!

Determined to dismantle the rollercoaster ride I had been living on for roughly seven years, I was excited to try and experience new things. No regrets, no looking back, I had made up my mind, I would rip the rearview mirror off of the car if necessary to have a new lease on life and focus on my future.

You need a fresh start! You deserve to be happy! Fuck the past, time to focus on yourself!

My transition started with job hunting. If I was going to be serious about starting over, I needed to cut several ties to my past and push forward in all aspects of my life. To my surprise, my new journey was going to move full steam ahead!

In a matter of 48 hours, I was enrolled in GED classes and had five job interviews. Penelope and I laughed uncontrollably about one of my interviews with a local partner for General Motors and Ford. This was an entry level position as a security guard. While the thought of me being a security guard and detaining someone was humorous, I had nothing to lose.

As I prepared for the interview with the security company, I reminded myself that this new opportunity wasn't

139

just about a job. It was more about me creating new surroundings, growing internally, and taking the necessary time to identify what I wanted in life.

One week into my GED classes and the first day of my new job, I was so excited. Life seemed a bit more advantageous than what I had been used to.

You got this girl, I thought to myself as I looked in the mirror, fixed my uniform, and pulled my hair up in a ponytail.

"Hey sis, are you excited for your first day? You look so damn cute!" Penelope said..

"Yes ma'am, I am going to rock the shit out of this day! I am so ready for a positive change."

"Who knew someone in a security uniform could be so attractive? Don't bring any stray's home." She said with a loud laugh

"I can't make any promises. Love you!"

I blasted my music all the way to work, trying to dance off all my nervous energy. I felt like a kid, getting ready for the first day of school. I was listening to KC and JoJo's album, *It's Real.* I can only imagine what the people driving past me we're thinking. Hell, I laughed at myself. I was putting on an entire concert in my car and cannot hold a tune to save my life. My first day was great, orientation went smoothly, and I was ready to go celebrate.

"Honey, I am home." I said, as I walked in the house.

My bestie was awesome, dinner was ready, and drinks were poured. We kicked it all night, talked about my new job, and how excited I was that my GED classes would be over at the end of that week.

"So, stop holding out," she said with excitement in her voice.

"What?"

"Really? You didn't meet one cute guy in the whole damn building today?

"I wasn't thinking about that, crazy. I was focused"

"Well, let's focus on getting you over Anthony and under someone else! I am just saying"

"That's it, you have officially lost your mind. Hand me another drink girl!"

Work continued to go smoothly, and I was overcome with joy to be meeting so many motivated people. My job was to scan the badges of employees and distribute guest passes. There were a few gentlemen who worked for a blueprinting affiliate within the building that came past my desk several times a day. They were always cracking jokes with each other and would stop to talk for a while.

Jamaine was the introvert of the two. He definitely did not seem as outgoing as his friend. Kyle was boisterous, always drawing attention to himself while Jamaine often stood quietly in the background. Jamaine stood five feet, six. His skin glistened like melting, dark chocolate. He obviously worked out. His chiseled frame was accentuated by his clothes. He was clean, sharp, and always professional. Unlike Kyle, Jamaine was extremely laid back, he carried a sense of confidence that almost made him appear arrogant. I was so attracted to how comfortable he was in his own skin. He made everyone in the room take notice, without saying a word!

***

"What a shame," Jae teased, shaking her head at me, and sucking her teeth as Jamaine and his friends walked away.

"Okay, what is the head shake all about?" I asked in an inquisitive voice.

"I saw the way you looked at him," she said with a devious smirk.

"Girl please. You didn't see anything."

"Whatever you say! Let me know if you change your mind, I have his number."

"If I was interested, I don't need help."

"If you say so. I think you both just need a good lay." She chuckled as she walked away.

Although I definitely was not looking for a new boyfriend, I thought to myself, *she might have a point. There isn't anything wrong with having a little fun!*

The next day when he came past my desk, I took advantage of the opportunity to make the conversation a little longer than usual.

"Good morning sunshine." I said with a flirtatious grin.

"Good morning."

"So, who is this beautiful baby you have posted on your cart?"

"My daughter. Jazmyn."

"She is so cute. How old?"

"Almost 2."

"Well, I am sure you and your girlfriend are very happy."

"Yeah, I am not with her mother."

"What a shame." I said with a seductive look.

"Not really." He turned and smirked as he walked down the hall.

I didn't get him to say much, but at least as I able to break the ice and get my foot in the door. Surrounded with a positive atmosphere, I was making new friends, starting to party less, and finally finishing school. There were just a few obstacles standing in my way. Anthony would not give up on trying to be with me and I continued to criticize myself with thoughts of self-doubt. Every time I started to get the nerve to talk to Jamaine a little more, my thoughts would start to get in the way.

Should I really say something to him? He seems like such a great guy! You do not want to fuck him up with your craziness. But he does look very appetizing!

A few days later I stopped Kyle as he walked past the desk, thinking I could feel him out a little and see what the playing field looked like with Jamaine. Just because he wasn't with his daughter's mother did not mean he wasn't involved with someone.

"Hey, can I ask you a quick question?" I asked with a nervous crack in my voice.

"What's up?"

"How well do you know Jamaine?"

"That's my boy, why? Oh, I see." He responded as he realized why I was asking.

"Jamaine is cool, he is really laid back. I don't think he has ever dated a white girl though."

Just then two other co-workers walked up. "What are we talking about?" Jae asked as she sat on my desk.

"Jamaine. From what I hear, he has never dated a white girl." I responded

"Wait now! I didn't mean it in a bad way. I was just saying I don't think he would." Kyle quickly said.

"Interesting. Is that a wager I hear on the table?" Jae asked.

"You girls are a trip. I am down for a bet. I don't think you can get him to go out with you though." Kyle said.

"Challenge accepted, what are the rules?" I asked with a look of determination .

"You can only go on a date. You can talk about anything, but you cannot have sex."

"Done! I will collect my $50 Monday morning sir."

My mind was racing with thoughts and excitement all the way home. I felt like a giddy little schoolgirl. My stomach filled with butterflies just at the thought of talking to him. As soon as I got home, I screamed for Penelope.

"Girl, you are never going to believe what I agreed to today?" I said with excitement.

"I am scared to ask. What?"

"I have to get this ridiculously sexy guy at work to go out with me."

"Okay. Why would that be a challenge?"

"He has never dated anyone white before and he has a one-year-old so there are probably some ties there."

"Good! Hell, that just means you can get some and be on your way." Penelope said, shrugging her shoulders.

"Well… that is one of the conditions of the bet. I cannot sleep with him. Not yet anyway."

"Tell me more. What does he look like?" She asked eagerly, plopping down on the couch, legs folded, and eyes wide open.

"Sexy as hell. He has shoulders that damn near bust out of his coat and the prettiest complexion. I can't focus when he walks past. I just want him to wrap his arms around me every time I see him."

I felt so girly and giddy as I described him. The more I said the rosier my cheeks became.

"Great! So, he is the complete opposite of Anthony's ugly, skinny ass. Thank God! I still don't know what the hell you were thinking," Penelope said with the utmost disgust in her voice.

"Funny, very funny!" I said, as I also often wondered what I was thinking.

"So, what is our time frame? How long before you can have sex and move on? Just asking for a friend." She said leaning her body in to absorb the details.

"I have a week, but it won't take that long." I replied with a wink.

***

In the days to follow, I went out of my way at work to extend our conversations from a simple hello to more personal topics. He seemed so bashful but was always willing to chat. By the end of the week, conversations started to become more natural. On Friday evening I stopped him on his way out of the building and decided to spice up the charm.

"Leaving so soon?" I said in a low voice as I brushed my body against his arm, spinning around, placing myself directly in his path. Standing face to face, captivated in each other's eyes.

"Yeah, how about you?"

"Shortly. What do you have going on this weekend?"

"Nothing, I will probably just hang out at home." He answered as he sized me up.

"Oh, I am sure you have someone to occupy your time." I responded as I thought to myself. *This is going to be fun!*

"Nope, it has been way too long since I have had any fun!" He said with a flirtatious smirk.

I intensely watched his mouth move, eyes twinkle, and the leather stretch tightly around his biceps as he adjusted his posture. As I started to speak my sigh resembled more like a moan, I could not stop myself from envisioning his arms wrapped tightly around my body.

Get yourself together! I thought, laughing internally.

"Really? I find that hard to believe. Anyway, I am not doing anything tomorrow. Interested in being bored together?" I said with a raised eyebrow.

"Okay, where and when?" He promptly answered.

"Pick me up at 7pm. Don't be late. I hate waiting!" I said with a devilish look as I handed him my address on a notepad.

Jamaine met me at my parent's house just to be safe. The knock on the door caught me by surprise. I expected him to call when he arrived. He carried himself as such a gentleman. Dad answered the door and invited him in, everyone introduced themselves and we chatted for a few minutes before heading out.

"Here, I will get the door for you!" He said, rushing to my side of the car to open the door.

As we started to pull out, I opened the conversation with a little humor to lighten the mood.

"So, this is new!" I said jokingly.

"What?"

"I have never known a serial killer that introduced himself to everyone in the family before running off with the victim."

From that moment, our conversation flowed so effortlessly. We laughed and talked about some of the most pointless topics. This was our first time seeing each other outside of work but it felt like we knew each other forever. Before the movies, he stopped at McDonald's to get something to eat. I could tell by his facial expression that he was looking for a negative reaction from me when he asked if I wanted something to eat.

"Hey, are you hungry?" He asked as he slightly looked at me out of the corner of his eye.

"No, I ate already." I said with a smile

He is so silly! He must be used to some superficial bitches!

After the movie, he took me back to my parent's house where we sat in the car talking for hours. We laughed about everything, talked about his daughter, and what we wanted out of life. As I was getting out of the car I leaned over and gave him a soft kiss goodnight. I did not expect just a gentle kiss to feel so passionate. As I looked deep into his dark, seductive eyes, I wanted to rip his clothes off and forget all about this stupid bet. But I couldn't, stay focused. My mind and body were in a full out war. One more soft kiss, as his hand caressed the side of my face.

"Have a great night!" I said with my eyes still closed and the taste of his lips still lingering on my mouth. Forcing myself to get out of the car, turning to take one more look at his beautiful face as my hand slid slowly and softly out of his grip.

"When can I see you again?" He asked.

"Monday, at work." I said glancing back with a smile as I walked in the house trying to pull my emotions together and stop the lustful thoughts racing through my mind.

I smiled all the way in the house. This feeling I had was different, although there was no denying the physical attraction we shared, I also longed for his conversation. Everything about Jamaine felt genuine. I knew he wanted me as badly as I wanted him, but there was more. Something beautiful, true, mysterious, and unforgettable. Every thought that penetrated my mind that weekend left me wanting to know more about him. Jamaine was my new distraction, a mystery I was determined to unravel.

How in the hell does such an innocent kiss have your mind racing?

As the days passed, my face continued to light up every time Jamaine was around. The sensation my body got was much more than a simple crush, he made me feel alive. I could be myself around him because there was no pressure to try and impress him. We were far past the silly bet and building a true friendship. We genuinely enjoyed each other's company and felt comfortable speaking freely.

No matter how welcoming he appeared, how comfortable my skin felt next to his, or how much I started to look forward to hearing his stupid metal cart coming down the hallway. I remained partially secluded to protect the remaining pieces of my heart. With time, my determination to isolate parts of myself was defeated by the attraction pulling me towards him. It was like there was a strong magnetic force pulling us together. I could feel "Blue-Eyes" waking up from her slumber but I couldn't risk going down that road again.

A full state of emergency was in effect. My mind was guarded and suited for battle, while my body was tiptoeing closer to the forbidden battle grounds with each thought of him. A soft whisper in my ear, over and over again reminding me that this was just a ridiculous bet that I took entirely too far. Soon my whispers became divided, one kind and hopeful voice begging me to release "Blue-Eyes" from the chains that held her captive for some long. The other doing whatever possible to toss painful memories back in the picture that made the possibility of Jamaine and I having something real hard to believe.

This battle within prevented me from giving my all to Jamaine but the undeniable passion kept pushing us together! We made sure we talked multiple times throughout the day and spent as much time together as possible. We made light of each other's heartbreaks and how naive both of us had been in the past.

Jamaine was on a journey of building a beautiful relationship with his daughter. While I was working on healing my soul. We were both trying to convince ourselves and each other that we were not interested in a relationship with titles. I think that is what made everything so effortless at first, we could lean on and confide in one another from the start without the complication of commitment. We were openly friends and lovers, no titles needed. At least that is the delusion that we made up in our minds.

"What is going on with you?" Penelope asked one day with an accusatory look on her face.

"I have no idea what you are talking about."

"Whatever! My girl finally got under someone! I am so proud of you." She said as she pushed my shoulder.

I just shook my head, chuckling as I walked out of the room. Jamaine brought true happiness to my life and the smile that covered my face every day was the evidence. The magic sparkling in my eyes was a result of pure desire, I was falling for him, and I didn't have to hide it this time.

Somewhere in the midst of all the late nights, and lack of titles, we struggled to spend even a day apart. All of our plans were made around each other's schedule, and I could see myself changing in ways I never did with anyone else. Girl's night out no longer lasted until 3am, and club night outfits no longer showed more skin than they covered.

After roughly five months of spending extended time together, I was offered a great job opportunity that was too good to pass up. Within the first two weeks of working my new schedule, it was evident that we didn't want to be apart.

Our phone calls got longer each night, weekend getaways were a built-in part of our lives, and each goodbye was harder to get through. Working separate schedules and living an hour apart made it impossible to see each other every day. We were always searching for ways to surprise one another or make any adjustment possible to allow for more time together.

***

I moped around the house, decorating for Penelope's surprise birthday. Upset that Jamaine was not going to make it due to his work schedule. We hadn't seen each other in almost a week and it was such a special night for my best friend and I really wanted him there with us. As the party took way, my friends tried to cheer me up.

"Girl, you will see him in a few days!" One of the girls said.

"Come on! I have something that will take your mind off Jamaine." Another one said as she wrapped her arm around my shoulder pulling me to the back room with them.

Penelope and I had just lined out cocaine on a mirror, and I was bent over in the process of sniffing a line through a rolled-up dollar bill when I became startled by a sound coming from behind me.

Creeeekkkk

As I heard the door open my heart dropped to the bottom of my stomach as Jamaine walked into the room, frozen, eyes bulging out of his head with shock.

"I can explain." I screamed, rushing quickly to the door. I was trembling inside with anxiety. I hadn't cared this much about another person's opinion in years.

"It's okay! This is your friend's night. We can talk about it later."

He hugged me and softly kissed my forehead, "I am going to go out here with the guys."

I was so nervous, beating myself up out of fear that I just fucked everything between us up. Until that moment Jamaine had no idea I did drugs. We shared many secrets with each other up until that point, but I was just too embarrassed about that part of my life. When I was with him, I didn't have the desire to drink or get high. I felt intoxicated just by being in his presence. Our connection brought me joy that I had never experienced. I feared this dark secret of mine would push him away.

"Hey, have you seen Jamaine?" I asked Marco as I anxiously walked around the house.

"Yeah, he left right after he went looking for you."

I frantically called him! My heart was beating so fast I thought it was going to come out of my chest. My hands shook in anxiety of what his reaction was going to be, but no answer. I sat on the end of the bed, trying to act like it didn't bother me that he left but I was devastated.

Heart racing, hands sweaty, and leg shaking uncontrollably, I realized I wasn't upset about being caught. I was mad at myself for letting him down; overtaken by the thought that I managed to pollute the one innocent, genuine piece of my life with my inability to control my impulsive addictions.

Oh Krissi! What did you do? I thought to myself as I paced the bedroom floor.

Ring... Ringgg

"Hello!" I said anxiously.

"Hey." Jamaine responded in a somber voice.

"What happened? Why did you leave?"

"I was just surprised. Why didn't you tell me? How long have you done that?"

"Longer than I'd like to admit. I never said anything because I did not want to push you away! And honestly, I didn't want to be interrogated about my poor choices."

"I don't want to be pushed away either, but I don't want to see you do that." He answered in a voice of despondency.

"Will you please come back?" I asked, sitting down on the bed. Impatiently awaiting his response.

"I will come and get you, but I don't want to be around the drugs."

"I will be ready when you get here. I am sorry for not telling you!"

As I rushed to pack an overnight bag I was petrified about the imminent conversation. Jamaine had no idea about any of the drugs let alone the amount of drugs I had been doing. He also had no clue of the depth of my alcohol abuse. I drank a little around him but only if there were other people drinking. At times I would pack vodka in my overnight bag and put it in my thermos like I was drinking water. Even this lessened the more we were together.

He did not drink or do drugs, he didn't even smoke. The time we spent together was purely about us. It felt good to not need or even desire those vices, at least while I was with him. Now, I had to own up to my truth and face the fact that I may have just pushed my only source of balance and structure away.

Jamaine and I talked for hours that night. I shared stories of trauma and details of my addictions that I vowed to never relive. As I laid wrapped in his arms, all I felt was love, compassion, and of understanding. It was then, I knew I was truly in love for the first time.

This is the man I was meant to marry! This is the missing piece to my puzzle!

"Don't cry! You have nothing to be embarrassed about. You are absolutely beautiful inside and out!" He whispered in my ear and kissed my forehead as he squeezed me a little tighter.

I had never felt this loved! Honest, unconditional love! I wanted to live in the moment forever, stay wrapped in his arms and feel the comfort of his pure compassion. As we embraced one another in intimacy, I felt more connected than ever before. As his hands moved down my spine and his lips on my neck, our night held more than just lust. Our embrace was spiritual. With each kiss, I became freer, with every touch of his hands I trusted him more, giving myself fully and completely to him. No more secrets, no more shame, I was madly in love. I found my prince charming.

Perhaps I had been wrong all this time and fairytales can come true!

A Fractured
Happily Ever After

The church continued to fill with family and friends, as chatter and giggles permeated the halls. I was in the dressing room spilling over with excitement at the thought of spending eternity with the man of my dreams! My hands quivered as I tried to apply eyeliner without making myself look like a raccoon. Penelope laughed as she picked up the makeup bag.

"You look stunning! I am so happy for you, see you upstairs!" She said with a smile as her and the other bridesmaids turned to head to the sanctuary.

"Are you ready honey?" My dad asked as he stepped into the dressing room.

"Yes sir!" My smile was big enough to cover my entire face.

I locked my right arm under my dad's and began to head up the steps. The sounds of Luther Vandross' *Here and Now* could be heard in every inch of the church. As we approached the sanctuary doors the song gracefully faded out as the doors slowly opened.

The song made a beautiful and subtle transition as the sounds of Jagged Edge *Let's Get Married* played in the background. I stood at the back of the sanctuary, eyes gazing forward until they met his. I took one step forward, and my knees started to shake, and my stomach felt tight. As I walked down the aisle, all I could see was Jamaine. The sounds of the music and vision of our guests were all blurred out in a hazy cloud. I grabbed my dad's arm tighter and took a deep breath. A tear crept out the corner of my eye as my body was overcome with happiness. I was no longer concerned about what the world had to offer or what tomorrow might bring. All that mattered was that I was going to spend each day moving forward with this beautiful man.

"Honey, are you okay?" My dad asked.

"Never better!"

So, this is what real love feels like!

With our hands intertwined, we exchanged vows,

"Kristina, repeat after me." The pastor instructed.

I couldn't wait to say the vows that would bind me to Jamaine for the rest of our lives. They were the sweetest words my mouth had ever spoken. With tears filling my eyes and my lips quivering. I began to speak.

"I, Kristina, take you Jamaine to be my husband. My best friend. My partner in life and my one true love. To have and to hold from this day forward. I will forever be there to laugh with you, to lift you up and to love you unconditionally through all the adventures of our life together. For better or for worse; for richer, for poorer; in sickness and in health. To love and to cherish, to comfort, encourage and inspire from this day forward until death do us part."

Once again, time seemed to escape me, but not like the traumatic times in my youth. This time, I was swept away in the pure ecstasy of the occasion. I looked down as Jamaine tenderly placed a ring on my finger. The church was filled with smiling faces and the sounds of all the women in the room sniffing as they wiped tears from their eyes.

All of this love for me? For us?

In slow motion, I heard the voice of the pastor say, "you may kiss your bride."

Jamaine and I shared the purest, most passionate kiss imaginable to seal our happily ever after, as he slowly wrapped his arm around my waist and dipped me backwards. The church was filled with applause as we were introduced as Mr. and Mrs. Quarles.

We danced and laughed the night away without a care in the world. Until this moment, I did not believe true happiness was obtainable. This type of love, the love I felt every time I even thought about Jamaine was only heard of in fairytales. As I sat at our wedding table smiling at him while he danced, I whispered a small prayer.

"Thank you, God, for allowing my fairytale to come true!"

***

Our journey together started out wonderfully. We both worked extremely hard, and Jamaine was in school. Our time was limited but we made the most of every minute. Jamaine helped balance me. Spending quality time together meant more to me than any party ever did. Drugs were soon far in my past and drinking was very minimal, only when friends came over. I always heard stories of how impossible it is to quit cold turkey, but for me it became another challenge I was willing to tackle.

I no longer needed alcohol to be my listening ear, to protect me when I felt vulnerable, or to give me boldness. Jamaine filled all of my voids. Partying with friends took on a whole new meaning, no drugs and loud music. Instead, the room was full of productive conversations, playing cards, and board games.

***

"Your skin is glowing. You just look different. Are you sure this is a stomach bug? Maybe you should take a pregnancy test!" My friend Roslyn asked.

"You are so silly. I am just sick." I responded nonchalantly.

"Well, being married looks great on you!" She said with a chuckle.

Although I laughed off her suspicion, her observations made me start to question my symptoms. I had been sick for a few weeks. I just imagined it was the flu or a cold. The possibility of me being pregnant never crossed my mind.

I never thought I wanted to be a mother. Hell, I never thought I would get married and find a purpose bigger than myself. Jamaine made me see life in a whole different light. My days seemed brighter and the nights so much warmer. He was an amazing father already. He loved being with his daughter, Jazmyn or "Jazzie" as I so affectionately called her. Jazzie and I bonded from the first day we met. We did everything together and I looked forward to spending time with her.

That night I found myself standing in the middle of Walgreens. My stomach was in knots as my eyes wandered aimlessly up, down, and across each shelf. I must have looked at 100 different types of pregnancy tests before buying three. I was so nervous as I walked into the bathroom, reading the instructions on each box like the way to pee on a stick was suddenly going to change!

Get it together before he gets home!

All three tests read positive. My body was overcome with emotion and confusion all at the same time. I rushed around the house cleaning and replaying how I was going to tell Jamaine we were having a baby!

Okay, do you just say it? Am I supposed to get him a card? Oh God, what if he doesn't want another baby?

In the midst of my frantic cleaning episode, I didn't realize he walked in the house until he wrapped his arms around me from behind.

"How was your day, wife?" he asked as he kissed my neck and gave my waist a squeeze.

"Better now!" I responded with a smile as I turned to face him.

"I have something to share with you." I muttered with a shaky voice.

"Okay. What's going on?"

I grabbed his hand and led him into the bathroom where all three tests laid in a row on the sink. As his eyes opened wide, my head tilted downward, peaking at him out of the corner of my eye to see his reaction. He immediately picked me up off the ground, squeezing me tight!

"I am so happy baby! You are going to be a wonderful mother" he said.

He seemed so confident in my ability to be a good mother. Although I was nervous, I knew I was going to give my baby the life and relationship I always wanted while growing up.

We were zealous to share the news with friends and family, but the excitement did not last long.

***

"That's strange" the nurse said under her breath, as she ran the transducer probe over my stomach frantically searching for something.

Jamaine and I looked nervously at each other. This was our first ultrasound, so we didn't know what to expect. I peered at the screen looking for the baby. I saw what looked like a dark shadow in the size and shape of a little pea. The nurse stopped, wiped the cold, gooey gel off of my stomach with a nervous reassuring smile.

"The doctor will be right in!" She said and marched out quickly. Although she remained professional, it was impossible for her to hide her concern.

Dr. Ryan came in with a look of desperation. Just a simple good morning was all he said. Forgoing the usual pleasantries, he squirted another glob of gel on my stomach and performed another ultrasound. I fidgeted with anxiety. Dr. Ryan was usually so talkative and personable, but today he was all business. Clearly trying to prepare himself to deliver troublesome news. My stomach felt like it was twisting in knots as I continued to stare at the screen while simultaneously watching his expression, searching for any sign of hope in his eyes. Sadly, with each stroke of the probe all I saw was growing despair.

"Are you experiencing any pain, Mrs. Quarles?" Dr. Ryan asked as he started to clean the gel from my stomach.

"Well, I am now. I'm a little nervous."

"I'm sorry to tell you this, but we could not find a heartbeat, and it seems your uterus is contracting. Unfortunately, you are having a miscarriage."

I was devastated. I couldn't speak. I just cried, eyes tightly closed, praying silently that I was in a dream. Jamaine squeezed my hand tightly as all his attention immediately turned toward my wellbeing.

"Are you sure?" Jamaine asked, trying to hide the pain in his voice.

"Yes, Mr. Quarles. I am very sorry!"

"How long does this process take? Is she going to be in pain?"

Dr. Ryan explained the process to us and put me on an IV to expedite the miscarriage and stop the pain. Things were happening so quickly that my mind seemed slow to catch up to what was taking place with my body! My fairytale was unraveling right in front of me. All of a sudden, I was catapulted back in time, sitting in the room telling the doctor about the rape, the untreated STD's, and the potential consequences.

In my mind, it was all connected. My poor decisions were destroying my happily ever after. It did not matter how much I changed or how deeply I fell in love with Jamaine and Jazzie, I could no longer run from my past. Jamaine knew about the rape, but we never discussed details including the STD's. I felt physically sick at the thought of looking the man that had given me everything in the face and telling him, this is all my fault!

This must be a cruel joke! How am I supposed to stay strong knowing I am the cause of this?

In less than 24 hours, my best friend, liquor was back in my hand, dulling the pain as I cried myself to sleep. The monsters were slowly creeping from under the bed, with whispers seeping from the closet. "Kristina" was back!

Walls were rapidly being rebuilt for extra protection. An internal storm was brewing out of control. Blue-Eyes was rushed back into captivity as the doubts of never being good enough for him or having a family grew stronger.

I could see the pain on Jamaine's face. He did everything in his power to keep it buried and be strong for us both. Fearful that my actions created the turmoil we were living in, I desperately continued to pretend I was okay.

While Jamaine drowned himself in work, I swam in liquor. My past had taught me nothing, I still lived with the delusion that Vodka was going to suppress the pain and guilt enough to move forward with no cracks in the foundations. Secretly my bitterness and thoughts of betrayal from God were seeping from every pore, brewing a strong intensity I had never faced.

How could I tell him that I was the reason his child didn't survive? How could I deal with the embarrassment of all of my poor irresponsible decisions? Decisions that destroyed the person I wanted to be and now held my future in its hands! Being strong, cold, and malevolent was the mask to hide my guilt, my only defense mechanism.

As I prepared for war, my beautiful little girl, Jazzie, reminded us brighter, happier times were possible. She was only five at the time but was able to bring life back to our darkness with just the sound of her laughter. I wanted to make sure every day she had with us was full of joy. No pain, no fighting, no tears, just her Daddy and Mommy K showing her what life should be. I would have done anything to protect her from what we were going through.

Our opposite work schedules made it easy for me to hide the alcohol abuse from Jamaine and force a smile on my face when he was home. Or so I thought! While I fooled myself into believing I had become a great actress, he was reaching out to a few of my friends concerned I was pulling away from him. Instead of taking the help that was right in front of me. I reverted to what I did best, I found distractions. I started working two jobs and even picked up some college classes. I started hanging out more and making sure I planned structured activities when Jazzie was home. I was willing to do anything to prove I was strong, I was not a victim, and I didn't need saving.

You have come way too far to look weak now!

My actions were almost robotic. I was planning and moving as if I had something to prove, never giving myself real time to grieve. Falling further and further into depression while becoming more isolated with each passing day. Jamaine wanted to be there for me so badly, but I just continued to close him out while I fostered a growing dependency on alcohol. My internal war continued to grow with thoughts of self-harm and negative self-reflection.

You can't hide from yourself! You are going to push him away just like you did Bee and Coi! You are so destructive, the only person you will ever be able to count on is yourself!

My personal tug-of-war game lingered for several months. As "Kristina" continued to overpower the cries of "Blue-Eyes" I was desperately looking for any sign of hope. Following the advice of Roslyn, I started to watch a few pastors on television when I was at home alone. Joel Osteen and Joyce Meyers.

Allowing myself to clear my mind enough to embrace their messages was more challenging than I imagined. I felt so angry and abandoned by God, that I wanted to preserve any part of the message that seemed to speak to me. Curled up in bed, liquor in hand and notepad next to me. I jotted down every word that translated to my story, my pain, reaching for any piece of God I could find. Each sermon ending with me asking the same question.

"Why did you leave me?"

During one of Joyce Meyer's sermon series that focused on overcoming pain and healing, it felt as if my father was in the room crying with me. An abundance of love controlled the room as I fell to my knees and cried out. With each word of the sermon spoken, life was restored back into my dying soul that day. As she delivered her message, I was reminded that our faith is going to be tested time and time again. The way we endure the test is based on our true measure of faith. My faith was fractured. I had misdirected my anger to the wrong people and

places, because my pain was misunderstood. I was searching for answers and reasoning to unfeasible circumstances.

The magnitude and depth of the test doesn't mean God
doesn't love us. It simply means the devil already knows
God's plans. One of the scriptures from the message stood
out in my mind, replaying like a flashing light!

"And let us not lose heart and grow weary and faint in
acting nobly and doing right, for in due time and at the
appointed season we shall reap, if we do not loosen and
relax our courage and faint." (Galatians 6:9 AMPC)

I was subdued by the desire to understand. Desperately
seeking answers, begging God to show himself to me.
This entire time I thought I was fighting, proving to the
world around me that I was strong. In reality, I was doing
the opposite of what scripture spoke. I wasn't standing
strong; I was giving up. The fracture of my faith was
spreading wide and long, stretching like a spider web
across my life. With each unanswered question the web
grew and with it the pain turned back to rage.

"I don't deserve to feel this way! I have tried to do so
much better for you, why don't you hear my prayers? God,
please answer me!" I cried aloud.

As my cries grew, the air in the room transformed, I no
longer felt alone. "Please answer me! I am begging you!"
I continued to cry.

Lost in my pleas, I didn't realize Jamaine came into the
room until he picked me up off the ground.

"I hear you baby, and God does too!" Jamaine said,
holding me close, wiping the tears from my eyes.

"I don't deserve you! You deserve to be happy and have a family!" I forced out as I gazed into his eyes. He looked so broken, lost in his desire to piece me back together.

"We are a family, together!" He replied, in a doleful voice.

We laid together in bed that night while I cried myself to sleep. Silent prayers that I would not wake opposed my desire to transfer all of Jamaine's pain to me. I was conflicted with emotion, unable to find the strength within to stand on my own two feet but determined to protect the love of my life.

***

Time seemed to slip by! Jamaine and I continued to thrive together, slowly picking up the broken pieces as our growing strength allowed us to mend the fractures and flawed lines. The bond Jazzie and I shared was priceless. She made me laugh more than I ever imagined possible. Witnessing the innocence, joy, and love this beautiful little girl embodied; helped me stand a little taller and provided me with a burning desire to try harder.

My daily purpose quickly moved from wanting to make it through the day, to a determination of making every moment count!

Jamaine was so romantic; he went out of his way to put a smile on my face. Waking me up in the mornings to rose petal walkways leading to bubble baths. Countless breakfasts in bed, and very well-planned date nights. His every move made me feel loved more and more with each passing day.

The tenderness I felt in Jamaine's arms made my flaws translucent. He saw me even when I wasn't trying to be seen, even when I went out of my way to be invisible and secluded; he still saw me! He looked past the superficial beauty. The basic and simplistic worldly expectations did not amuse him. Even before we became intimate, he saw me. The real me buried deep underneath all the pain and destruction. He was the only person that allowed me the freedom and security to slightly breathe enough for "Blue-Eyes" to reappear.

But just as quickly as my happiness came the devil stole it away with an unexpected gust of wind that ripped apart my beautiful family portrait.

Awakened by nausea, I sat still on our bed, fearful that the aching pains in my stomach were another painful memory of my past–a reminder that I was flawed beyond repair, and a fool to think someone so broken could ever sustain happiness. As I forced my legs off the side of the bed, the torn pieces of my magnificent family portrait slowly fluttered down around me, like leaves falling from a tree. A radiating pain shot through my back and down my legs as I stood to my feet, grinding my teeth, and bracing the side of the bed determined not to cry. The weight of my entire body rested on each leg as they lifted off the ground, each crippling step towards the bathroom sounded like the slow tapping of a bass drum. Stepping over the invisible reminders of what my family could have been, tormenting glimpses of pictures, and the haunting pitter patter of baby steps.

Oh my God, what am I going to say to Jamaine? God, why have you forsaken me again!

***

Palms sweaty and head pounding, I anxiously sat in the emergency room lobby waiting for my name to be called.

"Mrs. Quarles. Right this way please." My body jumped as one of the nurses called for us, holding the door for her colleague to push my wheelchair to our assigned room.

My heart was literally breaking as I was rolled down the hall, while I watched my husband trying to be a pillar of resilience. Pacing the floor of the hospital room, looks of exhaustion and hopelessness covered his body.

Knock, knock

"Hi guys. I am sorry we are seeing each other under these circumstances!" Dr. Anderson said, closing the door behind her.

She walked cautiously to the side of the bed, reaching her hand out towards mine. "I am so sorry you lost the baby!"

"What? I am not pregnant!" I said in anger, pulling my hand back as a river of tears poured down my face.

"Dr. Anderson, we didn't know we were expecting. We were concerned that this may be happening when she got sick but we did not know for sure." Jamaine replied as he sat on the bed next to me and wrapped his arms around my body.

"I am so sorry! The test results show you were between six to seven weeks along. There is nothing we can do. I am so sorry! Please rest and let me know if you need any-thing. We will have to do a procedure called a D and C before you go home to get rid of any abnormal tissues."

"Thank you!" Jamaine said as the doctor turned and walked out of the room.

My body fell flaccid onto the bed, "How is this happening to me again?!" I just laid there and cried. As my cries became more painful, I could feel each brick being added to another wall, as if I was picking it up and assembling the structure myself. Reconstruction was underway with vengeance. "Kristina" was taking control again. I laid in the hospital bed as only an image of the woman he loved. Underneath, my form was being twisted and turned, remodeled with a stronger frame, which soon would be unrecognizable.

You are never going to be able to make him happy! This is all your fault! You will never have a family with him!

"Baby, are you okay?" Jamaine said as I stared off into a daze.

"Baby!" He said again.

"I am sorry!" I replied in a cracked voice, unable to stop myself from crying.

"Stop it! This is not your fault. Please tell me you know that!"

"I just want to sleep." I said as I rolled over and waited for the doctor to come back and perform the procedure.

***

"Mrs. Quarles, how are you feeling?" Dr. Anderson asked.

"I am okay. Can we just get this over with?" I muttered, rolling back over.

"Of course!"

I laid watching the I.V. slowly drip, each drop reminding me of my imperfections, my shattered past. As my eyes became heavy and I struggled to keep them open, I replayed the night of the rape over and over again.

What did I do to deserve this? Why didn't I fight harder?

Continued thoughts of resentment, pain, anger, blame, and abandonment…until I awoke.

"Hi baby!" Jamaine said, squeezing my hand tighter while he leaned down to kiss me. I knew something was wrong by the look on his face. I had never seen Jamaine look so defeated and there was nothing I could do to take his pain away.

"Hi Mrs. Quarles. The procedure went fairly well but unfortunately there was extensive scar tissue covering your uterus and both fallopian tubes. Dr. Anderson continued to talk, but her voice faded out, and my body went numb. Jamaine caressed my hand and wiped the tears from my eyes. As my tears drenched my hospital gown, I felt another part of me drift away as my emotional cement hardened.

"The team worked diligently to remove as much scar tissue as possible, unfortunately your right fallopian tube is completely blocked. At this time, we are uncertain what this means for the possibility of pregnancies in the future. I truly wish I had better news for you both!" Dr. Anderson said, standing at the foot of the hospital bed unable to mask the pain she shared with us.

You have to leave him! You cannot make him happy!

"Mrs. Quarles, do you have any questions?"

"Mrs. Quarles?"

As I gazed up slightly making eye contact, I shook my head no. Quickly leaning over to Jamaine, "baby I just want to go home!" I said in a whisper.

"Okay!" He replied as he started to gather my things and helped dress me.

With the passing weeks I became so distant and mean. I found myself cutting our conversations short and avoiding any personal interaction. It did not take long before the compassion and desire I once had to protect my husband turned into bitterness and resentment towards myself. Here I was staring at this beautiful man that loved me more than life. But all I could see was my broken pieces scattered on the floor. With only a fraction of my heart remaining I had nothing left to give.

Even in these darkest hours, he accepted all my broken pieces and used his heart to make mine whole. Jamaine seemed to smooth all my rough edges every time I opened up and let him in. He always found a way to show me the best things in life are truly free, I never imagined I could love so deeply. Every relationship before him was based on control and adrenaline. Jamaine was and is my one and only real love. He taught me to love and waited for me to be willing to love him back, even in my weakest times.

***

We tried to go on with life like everything was fine and the pain was healed. For me, the pain was just buried with walls surrounding all the good pieces I had left. Over the next two years, Jamaine and I lost two more babies. Each loss was a reminder of my flaws, my weaknesses, and my inability to be loved, which resulted in me turning back to "Kristina" for protection.

You have been a fool! Stop wasting time on something that will never last! My world was literally disintegrating all around me; while the real me laid in a fetal position, covered with a bulletproof dome, doors chained and guarded.

Our third loss was quick, within a week of us finding out we were pregnant the baby was gone. I walked around the house like a zombie. Relying on cocaine and vodka to get me through the day. The only remaining pieces of my heart broke a little more every time I looked at my husband. I found myself hiding from the beautiful, loving face I once desired to see looking back at me. I couldn't bear the thought of hurting him anymore. For me, we had lost so much, all because of my poor life choices. I was the reason he was hurting, me staying with him would only result in more agony. He deserved to be happy and raise a family. He deserved to spend his days laughing, going to recitals, sharing family meals, and enjoying sporting events. He did not deserve to waste away trying to piece me back together. I was a lost cause, damaged far beyond repair.

You hear rumors that the first five years of marriage are the hardest. We embraced that with a smile and laughed like we were taking on the world. We could have never imagined that we would lose four babies in the first three and half years. There was nothing I could do to disguise the pain anymore. I fell further into depression and placed all of my focus on my addictions.

The fourth loss hit the hardest. Due to the number of losses, we were considered high risk and had weekly visits with the OBGYN. As our eighth week arrived, a huge sigh of relief came over both of us.

This time is going to be different! It has to be!

Week nine visit went smoothly!

"Mr. and Mrs. Quarles, everything looks great so far. Try not to stress about hearing the heartbeat, it can be faint this early on depending on the baby's positioning. Get some rest and we will see you next week."

"Thank you so much!" I said trying to contain my elation as I took the ultrasound pictures from the doctor.

The car ride home seemed less stressful than weeks past. I even found the energy to laugh while I looked at my loving husband and said,

"You are truly my best friend. I don't know why you have stayed with me through all of this, but I am forever grateful! I don't know what I would do without you!"

"I don't know what I would do without you!" He responded as he softly kissed my hand.

***

Wake up! Please Wake up!

I cried softly as I cradled myself into the fetal position so he wouldn't hear. In too much pain to get out of bed, I tried everything to maneuver my body without waking him up.

This cannot be real!

I rolled myself out of bed as quietly as possible and crawled to the bathroom. Slowly pushing the door closed and pulling myself up on the toilet. I tried to muffle my cries by covering my mouth with one hand as I realized I was drenched in blood.

God! Where are you?! Why do you keep leaving me?!

"Baby, are you okay?" Jamaine said as he lightly knocked on the door.

"No!" I cried out as I tried to catch my breath.

The bathroom door flew open, "Baby it is going to be okay. I promise." Jamaine sighed in disbelief as he rushed to grab towels and lifted me in the tub. "Everything is going to be okay."

God, I cannot handle much more! Why does this keep happening to me? What did I do?

"Yes, I understand. We will head that way now." Jamaine said as he hung up the phone.

"Baby, let me get you dressed. Dr. Anderson wants us to meet her at the hospital." He said as he helped me out of the shower.

I didn't speak the entire ride to the hospital. My tears continued to fall like rain, my shirt was so wet as tears continued to fall. I didn't have the energy to wipe them away, I just let them fall while I rubbed my stomach.

"Mommy loves you so much buddy, please try to hold on for me!" I repeated over and over in a low voice.

"We are almost there! I love you so much, please don't leave me!" I muttered as my cries got louder.

Jamaine rubbed my left leg with his hand while he drove, not saying a word. I could tell by the look of emptiness on his face, he was holding back his tears for me. We went into the emergency room where we were greeted by Dr. Anderson's nurse.

"Come with me Mr. and Mrs. Quarles, we have a room ready upstairs." she said, sadly.

The hallway seemed long and the elevator ride seemed even longer. I sat in the wheelchair, rubbing my stomach with all the wonderful plans I had for this beautiful baby falling apart like confetti in my mind. My legs were shaking, and my body felt cold. I suddenly got so tired I could barely hold my head up.

"Hi Mr. and Mrs. Quarles, let's help you up on the table and see what is going on." Dr. Anderson said in a compassionate tone.

My body shivered as she placed the ultrasound jelly on my stomach. My adrenaline was at a monumental high, I held my breath anticipating her expression to change as the probe slid across my stomach.

"Can you get an IV started and let's run some labs?" She said to the nurse.

"Mr. and Mrs. Quarles, I am so very sorry! There is nothing we can do to save the baby; the placenta has ruptured, and it appears the fetus is attached to the fallopian tube wall. You have lost a tremendous amount of blood. I can only imagine how painful this is for you both, but we have to get you to surgery right away. If we don't we'll be putting your life in jeopardy as well."

I couldn't speak, I couldn't even nod my head. I just wanted to die at that moment.

No surgery, just let us both die!

"Mr. and Mrs. Quarles, there are some forms we need you to sign saying you understand the surgery will terminate the pregnancy." One of the nurses said as she handed Jamaine a clipboard and pen.

"Baby, everything is going to be okay!" Jamaine reassured me, as he signed the documents and handed me the pen.

I just scribbled something on the papers, I didn't read them or even look down to see if I was on the right line. My body was lifeless to its surroundings. I felt like I was in a daze as the room became foggy.

"Someone call the doctor quickly; she is passing out!" I vaguely heard and then there was darkness.

My eyes were so heavy, I tried to open them but all I could do was squint. Struggling to reposition my body, I noticed my legs wouldn't move. Glancing over to the right, I saw the IV still in my arm and the sounds of the monitors chirping like birds.

"Baby" I said quietly, lacking the strength to raise my voice, experiencing the worst headache imaginable.

I glanced down, noticing his head resting on the bed, hand over mine. I cried at the look of exhaustion on his face. Not saying a word, trying not to wake him. Overcome with fear of what the doctor would say when she came into the room.

"Hi Mrs. Quarles, how are you feeling?" The nurse asked as she checked the machines in the room and changed the IV bag.

"I am really sore, and my legs feel heavy."

"Let me get the doctor, she wanted to know as soon as you woke up." she responded and quickly walked out of the room.

Jamaine jumped up and kissed me all over my face, "I am so glad you're awake." He said as he tried to hold back a tear.

"What happened? What did they do? I don't remember anything!" I said in a panic.

"Let's wait on the doctor." he said as he sat back down and grabbed my hand.

I quietly laid in the hospital bed, staring at the ceiling while I anxiously awaited the doctor's arrival. Jamaine's hands still over mine with his elbows rested on the mattress. His body looked drained of all emotion, skin flushed, eyes puffy and bloodshot from lack of rest.

"Good morning Mrs. Quarles, how are you feeling?" Dr. Anderson asked as she approached the foot of the bed.

"Good morning, I am just really sore and tired."

"There is no easy way for me to say this! When we got you into the surgery there was more damage than we anticipated. Your right fallopian tube was ruptured as well as your right ovary. We had to fully remove both. While we worked as quickly as possible there was too much damage to the left side to completely repair it. We tried everything we could without putting you at any further risk. Your left fallopian tube is blocked and your uterus has a significant amount of scar tissue......"

My mind drifted as Dr. Anderson continued to explain the details of my horrific surgery. Soon her voice seemed far off in the distance although I could still see her blurred image at the foot of the bed. As the room came back into focus, her voice got louder.

"......I know this is difficult to hear and I am so sorry for your loss. Unfortunately, due to the damage to your reproductive organs if you continue to try and have children your husband could possibly be forced to make the decision to save you or the baby. Due to the amount of blood loss we had to make an incision through the abdomen, that is the pressure you are feeling. We will need you to try and get up to walk later today but take your time. You lost a lot of blood. Do you have any questions for me?"

I just stared straight through her as Jamaine responded for us both, "No, thank you so much for everything!"

"I am truly sorry for your loss!" Dr. Anderson responded as she turned to walk out of the room.

Over the next few days I regained my strength and was able to discharge home. I should have felt loved with so many people reaching out and asking if we were okay. I instead felt overwhelmed and pitiful. I worked so hard to put on a brave face and show everyone I was strong enough to handle whatever storm came my way. But all the smiles, thank you, and yes, we are going to be okay replies were simply for show. I was dead inside! Just a fragment of what I desired to be for Jamaine, what he deserved in a wife and best friend.

I found myself barely talking to Jamaine, drifting further into seclusion. I was too embarrassed to look my husband in the eyes. Every time I saw his face and felt his kiss, I just wanted to apologize for breaking our family. I prayed day and night for God to give me a reset button, just one more chance to get it right.

I just need one more chance God!

Unbreakable

I struggled to find a reason to wake up in the morning and the strength to move forward. I spent the next few months engrossed in bitterness and anger, most of which came pouring out on my sweet husband every time the pressure was too much to bear.

I laid on the couch one evening waiting for Jamaine to get home from work. Silently crying to myself, praying for a glimpse of hope in the middle of this nightmare.

How did we get here? How do I fix this for us?

As Jamaine walked in the house, he kneeled down beside me and kissed my forehead.

"Baby, I can't do this anymore! Everywhere I look I see pain and loss. I feel like I am falling apart again. I am scared I am not going to be able to get back up this time." I whispered as tears started to roll down my face and I gently grabbed his hand.

"I just want you to be happy! I want us to be happy!" I cried.

"We will figure this out together! I promise." he said as he walked to the bedroom.

A few days passed and I was trying desperately to get my game face on while I packed to go to Jamaine's family reunion in Tennessee. It had only been roughly three months since the surgery, and I was very hesitant to be in mixed company. Especially company I did not know very well.

It will be good to get out of the house! You have to try for him!

The seven-hour drive was peaceful. No responsibilities, no deadlines to meet. Just him and I, holding each other's hands, with little to no words. In that quietness a sense of ease came over me. I can't explain how or why, but as the breeze hit my face through the open window, I knew we would be okay at least to get past this roadblock.

There is something powerful that happens when you are able to trust the process. Through all of our pain, the one thing I kept being reminded of, was that I cannot control everything that happens. I can only continue to work on my healing and better guide my reactions to the undesirable situations that occur.

***

Our visit with his family went pretty well. I was finally able to relax and take my mind off of everything back at home. It was evident that we both seemed happier outside of our normal surroundings. Disconnecting ourselves from the consistent reminders of loss started to open the door for healing.

"What are your thoughts about starting over somewhere new?" Jamaine asked.

"Are you serious?" I responded with a smile big enough for our family back in Michigan to see.

"Yeah, I think it would be good for us all the way around! All I want to do is make you smile like this all the time!"

"I would follow you anywhere! You are my everything!" I said as I grabbed his face and gently kissed his lips.

"We are going to be okay baby!" He softly whispered as he wrapped his arms tightly around me and lifted me off the ground, kissing my neck.

Our mind was made up, a fresh start it was! We both applied for jobs and looked at apartments in Tennessee. Within three months, we were all packed, and on the road, to start our next chapter.

Our transition went smoothly, we were both adjusting into work quickly and making new friends. However, it did not take long before us working opposite shifts allowed my mind to wander and the depression that I swept under the rug to creep out. It's funny how we think we can run from the challenges we face in life. Just pick up and start over, everything will be fine.

I smiled as I stood in the mirror, trying to convince myself I was okay for months. The thing is, we cannot hide from ourselves. Every time you stand in the mirror, the pain that you refuse to address is staring back. With no proper guidance and lack of trust in those around me, I quickly turned back to drugs and alcohol to calm my mind while Jamaine was at work.

Even after being over 700 miles away from the people that knew me best, and partied with me the most, my past still had a hold on me. I managed to attract individuals who struggled with depression and addiction, just like me. Before I could blink, I was using cocaine multiple times a week and back to drinking vodka like it was water. The only thing that stopped me from completely going over the edge of the nearest cliff was the thought of breaking Jamaine's heart.

You are going to break his heart when he finds out! You can't hide this forever!

***

I sat on my knees crying on the living room floor, three things sat in front of me. To the left was a mirror filled with perfectly divided lines of cocaine. Directly in front of me was a pile of ultrasound pictures, harsh reminders of the love that would never come to pass. To the right of me was a bottle of Percocet and a bottle of vodka. With each glance of the ultrasound picture my heart broke a little more. When tears fell another line was snorted. Washing down the after taste of cocaine in my throat with pure vodka. The room became a blur, just fantasies flashing before me as I used my finger to outline each image on the ultrasounds, imagining the light touch of my finger mixed with my tears would magically bring life back to the departed.

Before I knew it, the sun had risen and there was no time to hide my little secret, nor the energy it would have required to clean my mess before Jamaine got home.

Cling...cling

I could hear the metal of the key turning in the lock, but my body no longer possessed the strength to lift or turn my head in the direction of the door.

"Baby, how can I help?" Jamaine asked in the most compassionate tone as he kneeled in front of me.

I could not answer. The only energy that remained was just enough to allow tears to roll down my face as my body fell into his arms. As he picked me up off the floor, I allowed my body to collapse against his. I was so tired. However, the mixture of substances within me made it impossible to rest. As he laid me on the bed, the room shifted in and out of focus with hallucinations of a baby crying in the background.

God please make it stop! I prayed to myself as I aggressively wiped my eyes in an attempt to bring the room into focus.

"I am so sorry! I just don't know how to move forward!" I cried out in pain.

Jamaine just kissed me on the forehead and gently laid my body on top of his. Chest to chest, allowing my heartbeat to mirror his.

"I don't deserve you!" I whispered as I started to doze off to sleep, body completely relaxed.

"I don't deserve you! You are so much more than the pain we have been through! I just need you to see what I see!" He responded as he held me close in his arms.

***

As my battle within continued to grow, I looked for everything I could to keep me busy. Reverting back to that 14-year-old little girl, searching for any escape possible. Anything to take the pain away, anything to occupy my mind, anything to make me feel whole.

I picked up extra shifts at work and volunteered at a local church that often supported events with the company I worked for. Although I eagerly desired to fill my time, I was hesitant to invest any part of me in the church. I was still angry with God, there were too many unanswered questions and a lingering sense of abandonment. I was a lost soul. I was unwanted by my earthly parents and unheard by my heavenly father. Walking into church would be like prancing into my enemy's house, so I thought.

Pushing my hesitancy aside, I remained committed to my volunteer engagements and soon developed strong relationships with some of the church members that urged me to attend a Sunday service. Jamaine and I had not been very disciplined in attending church services thus far in our relationship. Although I continued to follow Joyce Meyers and Joel Osteen, most of my spiritual connection came from personal talks with God while I was alone.

There was something different about this church, something that grabbed my attention even as I drove past it on my way to work.

Maybe I will be relaxed enough to hear God if I go. Maybe God will finally hear my pleas.

A few weeks later I was tossing around the idea of going but Jamaine's schedule never seemed to line up with mine. One Saturday night I became so restless out of the blue. My anxiety was at an all-time high. As I poured a glass of vodka, I suddenly lost the desire to drink and picked up a journal I started writing in, a few years earlier.

This journal was a method of release for me after the loss of our children. I would write notes explaining how I felt and every little thing I wish I could have said to them. I started to cry as my hand brushed over the pages, outlining each sentence of our journey.

To my precious angel. You will never know the dreams I had for you, the joy I felt even at the thought of hearing your coo. I have to believe that God had a bigger purpose for you and me both. Mommy just can't seem to stop searching for the why's in the unknown! I feel as if I said goodbye as quickly as I said hello to you and your siblings. Such an unfair feeling and a wound unable to heal. I pray for you each and every night. I pray that your soul is dancing with your uncle and grandfather. Free of pain, sickness, and disease! So tonight, as I search for my purpose, I pray for the strength to accept God's plans and trust the unknown. Rest peacefully my love, while I dream of how beautiful your wings are and how magical your presence must be in heaven.

Until we meet again,

Love Mommy

"I am so sorry I could not save any of you!" I spoke out loud as I prayed their little soul found rest.

Lying in bed, hypnotized by the rotation of the ceiling fan, the energy in the room shifted. A soft breeze gently blew by as a familiar aroma filled the air. The same aroma that lingered in our family living room as my dad started to weep and beg for forgiveness.

Thank you for showing yourself! Silently saying to God.

Sunday morning, I stared in the mirror with thoughts of frustration and embarrassment about my past traumas and my current substance abuse.

The whole damn church is going to catch on fire when I walk in... I thought as I tossed clothes around the room.

I can't do this alone!

"Good morning sunshine! Any chance you would want to try out this church with me today? It is over by my house, Cornerstone." I said to my friend Trish.

"Sure, I have been thinking about going there for a while now. Do you want to ride together or meet at the church?" She responded quickly

"We can meet there. I will call you when I am in front of the church. Thanks!" I answered with a sigh of relief.

I apprehensively finished getting ready, changing my outfit a dozen times before rushing out the door. As we walked into the church, I was amazed at how big the sanctuary was and how friendly everyone seemed. The staff greeted us, but to my surprise it was more than a simple hello. The tall slender gentleman promptly asked us if we were new to the church.

"Yes sir." Trish and I both responded.

"Well, we would love the opportunity to share some information with you over coffee following service. What do you say?" He said in an antistatic voice.

"I would love to!"

"Great! My wife and I will meet you at the coffee shop right around this corner following service. My name is Jim by the way!" He said with excitement as he helped us find a seat.

As we took our seats, dulcet, enticing music slowly played throughout the church. The melodic sounds lifted and became richer as each instrument strategically fell perfectly in place, creating a sonorous tone.

The sounds of the drums magnified, allowing majestic imagery to manifest in our minds as the choir gracefully blended in and the choir director started to speak words of encouragement over the congregation.

"Merciful Father, we pray today that our minds are open, and hearts are healed! We offer ourselves to You

freely and trust You to be our guide, the director of our hearts, the forgiving author of all hope, and the object of true love. We come today seeking peace and healing. Shower us with Your mercy and grace, striking all fear, anxieties, and doubt from our souls. Grant us a quiet mind, receptive heart, and great expectation. For by Your grace the battle is already won! Hallelujah!"

The voices of the choir lifted in beautiful unison; each word being raised higher in convocation. *"Take back what the devil stole from me, and I rejoice today. For I shall recover it all. Yes, I rejoice today! For I shall recover it all!"*

The atmosphere became freeing as an undeniable anointing covered the room. The pastor followed praise and worship with a breathtaking message of forgiveness and accepting what we cannot change nor control. I spent the next hour and a half soaking in as much information as possible.

"What we fail to understand is the meaning of a real relationship with God. One that does not consist of the outfit you have or the job title you hold. A relationship built on trust and standing on a foundation of commitment. We must be committed to our healing and trust God to be in control. The human desire to be in control is rooted in a lack of faith. Without faith we are walking through life wearing a blindfold, living in misery, and expecting the worst.

Proverbs 4:25-27; Let your eyes look straight ahead, fix your gaze directly before you. Give careful thought to the paths for your feet and be steadfast in all your ways.

Do not turn to the right or the left, keep your foot from evil.

We must stop looking around trying to figure things out on our own. There is only one way home, and it does not consist of going backwards!"

The pastor closed service with a beautiful prayer over the congregation as the band played behind him. He encouraged anyone present that had a special need to talk to God, a prayer that needed the support of two or more, and anyone simply needing to feel loved; to come to the front of the sanctuary and pray with the elders of the church. I felt a tingling sensation as if the pastor was speaking directly to me.

As I made my way out of the aisle and to the front of the sanctuary, my knees began to buckle and my hands became clammy.

"Hi young lady! My name is Sister Blanch. Don't be embarrassed about anything. The Lord says when two or more are gathered prayers are heard and answered!" She said in an empathetic voice as she grabbed my hands.

"Hi! My name is Krissi. I struggle with addiction and have for several years. I have so much pain!" I responded with a quavering voice.

"My love, your spirit may feel broken, but it is not your burden to carry! The Lord will heal your wounds and take away your pain. You only have to ask and surrender the load! Let's pray!" She said with a smile.

My body slightly jerked, and I quickly opened my eyes as she began to pray. I had only heard of people being gifted to pray in tongues. I had never witnessed it firsthand. The longer she prayed, I felt a warm vibration radiate from her body to mine as a breeze came over the room. You could feel the loving connection growing with every sound she made. My body tensed up as she pulled me closer to her,

"Relax my child! Allow God into your soul and mind. Release these burdens for they are not yours to bear!"

For a moment in time, I felt a glimpse of hope and freedom. I envisioned a world with laughter and joy, a life where I had never been hurt, abandoned, and taken advantage of. A world where the pain was finally gone and the anger I felt related to my past and our losses was no longer controlling my thoughts.

"Trust the Lord my dear. You are His and He is yours!" She whispered and then transitioned back to praying in tongues.

The sanctuary was still filled with people, but as I relaxed my body and mind all I felt was the presence of Sister Blanch and God.

I went to meet with Jim and his wife Sue following the service. We talked for hours about what classes the church had to offer, including support groups. I was so intrigued by Jim's walk with God. He opened up about his drug addiction and even shared details of when he finally hit rock bottom. Jim shared a quote with me that day that has replayed in my mind for years.

We cannot go back and change the beginning of our journeys, but we can be willing to start where we are and rewrite our endings. The choice is completely ours.

—*C.S. Lewis*

***

For the next few years my walk with God was a roller coaster ride, but I was committed to every step. I started attending Wednesday classes, never missed a Sunday, and volunteered with every event that my schedule allowed. Within a year of becoming a member of Cornerstone, I joined the choir. My participation with the choir allowed me to build more of a personal relationship with a very diverse crowd of people, from all walks of life.

I was growing stronger with each passing day. While I still battled with alcoholism, I was no longer turning to drugs to calm my storm. My faith grew by watching the people around me transform. I was surrounded by people that had a history of drug abuse and a pastor that served a prison sentence for murder. They were all the most compassionate people I ever had the privilege of meeting. They all possessed an undeniable love for God, blind faith, and a divine dedication to saving souls. When my trials became too much to bear, for once I was able to see the light at the end of the tunnel. My salvation no longer seemed doomed.

If God can forgive them, surely, he can forgive me!

In October of 2007, our church held a women's retreat. The retreat was scheduled to focus on healing and the power of forgiveness. A four-day venture away from the world. We would all be camping, no phones, no televisions, just fellowship and worship. Some of the choir members and Trish continued to encourage me to participate, but I was very hesitant. I had never been camping and I am terrified of bugs. The Wednesday class and sermon for the week leading up to the retreat focused on taking control of our own destiny. That Sunday, the pastor recited something that moved my soul.

Your focus guides your emotions, emotions direct your behavior, behavior determines result, results control outcomes, and outcomes control our destiny. Ultimately, you can control your destiny by controlling your focus!

-Unknown

That sermon was the nudge I needed to take some positive personal time and go on this retreat.

The following Thursday, I headed out for the retreat. I was excited and nervous all at the same time. I still felt out of place, I didn't have a formal way of prayer, I simply talked to God as if we were holding a conversation. The most I could tell you about the Bible was related to Noah's ark or Jonah in the whale. Not that I truly understood the meaning behind either story, I just remembered hearing them as a child.

Listening to Joyce Meyers and Joel Osteen was more inspirational to me than reading the Bible. Their sermons seemed therapeutic. Placing me in the setting of emotional support and understanding versus me being concerned I would be judged because I could not tell you where a specific scripture was or recite one. I earnestly prayed that our women's retreat would not feel like a test on biblical knowledge.

The next four days were full of exciting workshops focusing on mental health, positive thinking, forgiveness, and self-love. I was motivated by the structure of the retreat and how interactive each workshop was. Sharing details of my pain, trauma, loss, drug addiction, and alcoholism was freeing. There were no wandering eyes or whispers as I shared my stories, just love and reassurance.

I grew saddened by the close of the weekend. I had gained so much positivity and wholeness out of the experience. I didn't want the feeling to end. The last night of the retreat was our dedicated time for reflection and our "Nail it to the cross" workshop.

For this workshop all the elder women of the church came to the campground and guided us through a beautiful set of activities. As we sat in our room waiting to get started, the air in the room shifted. My stomach dropped and my arms were covered with chills. I looked up and noticed our elders coming in together. They were all poised with such confidence and self-assurance regarding their relationship with the Lord. I didn't know any of their personal stories, but I wanted to hold the same dedication and closeness that they had when it came to my journey with the Lord.

They told the story of Jesus washing the feet of His disciples, as one by one the leaders of the retreat came around and washed the feet of us first timers. I was caught a little off guard and amazed by what some may see as a simple act, yet was so powerful. This act was my proof that I was not alone, my past does not define me, and there was a much bigger purpose for my life!

As the "Nail it to the cross" workshop started, we were all handed small square pieces of paper. Our instructions was to write down areas of our life we needed to let go of and trust God to control. I sat and stared at my stack of papers, still hesitant to let the walls down. Once again, I felt my angel on one shoulder, begging me to release

"Blue-Eyes" and find peace. While my devil stood strong on the other shoulder, questioning everyone's motives.

Am I really ready to let these people in? Oh my god, what if this is a trick and I have been misled? What if this is a cult?

These walls had been my security blanket for so many years. With "Kristina" protecting us from all perceived threats.

Is it really safe? How can I be certain these people can be trusted?

As these thoughts raced through my head. One of the leaders walked over and sat next to me.

"I struggled to let people in at first too! I thought I had it all figured out. If you don't let anyone in, you can't get hurt. Trust me, we hurt ourselves more when we try to do everything alone! Just write one down. I promise you will feel better!" She said with an angelic voice as she slid a small square paper in front of me and stood to walk away.

I tapped my pen on the table about a dozen times, staring at all the paper squares. As I reluctantly started to write, before I knew it the words and emotions just started to follow.

Pain over trauma, addiction, loneliness, control, shame, doubt, fear, bitterness, jealousy, depression, and lack of faith.

My thoughts poured out on paper and the tears poured down my face. These were not tears of sadness. They were tears of relief! I was so scared to move forward on this new journey. Honestly, I didn't want to look in the mirror and believe I was okay with not carrying a baby and raising a family. I wasn't sure I was ready to let go of the pain, anger, and bitterness. Part of me was comfortable in the pain, it was a familiar place to be. A place I learned to accept as long as "Kristina" was manning the gates.

By nailing these words on the cross. I was agreeing to start a new path. A path where "Blue-Eyes" was no longer in hiding and fear of the unknown did not control my movements and emotions. One by one we each took turns nailing our squares to this 12-foot cross handmade by the male elders of our church using two-by-fours. As each woman walked to the cross you could feel the love in the room grow with intensity, as the woman that went before handed off the hammer and nails to the next in line! The air seemed lighter, and the wind blew a soft breeze through the tent covered room. It was evident God's presence was near!

I felt a lump in my throat and knots in my stomach as the hammer was handed off to me. I slightly put my head down as I began to walk towards the cross.

"My dear! You have nothing to be ashamed of and you have nothing to fear! There is no judgment here. The Lord knows all of our secrets and insecurities. You are a child of God and a blessing to us all! We are all here to support you on this journey. We are all your sisters; you never have to feel alone again!" Sister Dana said, as she held her hand out to mine.

We walked to the cross together, hand in hand. I kneeled down, placing my squares on the ground near my feet. As I picked up the hammer and one piece of paper, Sister Dana handed me my first nail! I felt so loved, so supported, so protected, and so blessed to be in this moment. This is the first time since childhood that I felt safe to show the person I truly was. To be completely vulnerable, no secrets, no missing pieces to the puzzle, no "Kristina" manning the gates. With every swing of the hammer another wall came crashing down! My heart began to beat faster and faster as each nail cracked through the wood of the cross. As tears were released, they were met with broken wood landing on the cross. The sounds of the wood breaking echoed in my ears. With each paper square added to the cross, I felt a weight lifting off of my body as if it was being carried out of the room by a force more powerful than me.

My tears were a sign of rebirth! I was rejoicing in the thought of happiness and freedom. Freedom from pain, sorrow, guilt, shame, resentment, and unforgiveness. Freedom from every dark, unrelenting emotion, that I pushed down over the years. As I handed the hammer and nails off to the next women in line. It was not the broken and damaged Krissi passing the hammer on. Instead, the hammer was being held by this loving, beautiful, kind, caring spirit, named "Blue-Eyes"!

***

The room continued to fill with the anointing of the Lord as each woman nailed their pains and burdens to the cross. We cried together; arms linked showing how much we supported each other's journeys. While we were all overflowing with the Lord's love and soaking up the atmosphere, the elder women of the church were busy gathering at the front of the room.

"Ladies, can we ask you to join us please? Everyone take a seat. We have something special we would like to share with you!" Sister Dana said with excitement in her voice.

All the folding chairs had been rearranged into aisles. The tables were folded and pushed to the side. As we gathered and took our seats, everyone was facing the front of the room where the elder women stood. There was an infectious energy in the room and an aura surrounding the elders as they gracefully stared into the crowded room with glowing smiles on their faces.

"The Lord has reminded us today that our work here is not yet done! Our hearts and minds are overcome with joy as we see the changes in each of you that have occurred over the last few days. The transformation that took place this evening, poured out love and forgiveness like we have never seen before! God is busy at work!" Sister Brittany said.

"As we come around, if you are tapped on your shoulder, please take a seat at the front of the room!" Sister Dana said, as a selected few elders started to walk around, graciously moving from aisle to aisle.

As I looked around examining the room, I felt a subtle tap on my right shoulder. I gazed up making eye contact with one of the elders. She gently nodded her head yes as I anxiously stood, body still processing the emotions from nailing all of my small squares to the cross. My knees still a bit wobbly and hands shaky as I approached the front of the room.

"Release your burdens unto the Lord! He doesn't want you to hold this guilt, shame, frustration, and unforgiveness in your hearts!" One of the elders cried out.

I stood facing the front of the room as the leaders of the retreat started to softly sing, *Faithful is Our God.* Sister Blanch stood in front of me, another elder standing to each side of her helping her maintain her posture. I nervously began to sing along.

"I am reaping the harvest God promised me. Take back what the Devil stole from me, and I rejoice today for I shall recover it all!"

With my eyes tightly closed, Sister Blanch gently placed one hand on my forehead and the other on my stomach. She slowly started to pray in tongues, with each spoken word, her voice projected louder and louder until the room was filled with all the elder women praying and the sounds of the retreat leaders' cries were heard. As Sister Blanch pulled me closer to her, I could feel the energy surrounding her cover my body as if it was forming a bond around the two of us.

"My child, your pain radiates with a powerful anger and rage. Such sadness and sickness are not yours to bear. Do not mourn your losses. For God has a greater purpose for all that has happened! Trust the Lord, a miracle that will exceed glorious expectations is in your path. You will raise beautiful men of God! Trust the Lord with all you have, my precious child!" She quietly spoke as she wrapped her hands around mine, lifting them to my chest.

"You are more than what you seem! Your purpose is greater than you could imagine, and you are loved more than you'll ever know. The enemy is going to throw obstacles in your path full of lies and deceit. Continue to seek the Lord with all your heart and find your way home! The victory will be yours!" Sister Blanch prayed over me as she released my hands and stepped back to her seat.

As she stepped away, I fell to my knees. My body still felt as if it was surrounded by an anointing. My mind started to race with confusion.

How did she know about the losses? How did she know about all the pain?

I had prayed with Sister Blanch in the past for healing over my addiction but never disclosed the losses of our children or the sickness my family suffered.

How could she have known? What guided her hand to my stomach?

It was evident, God was undoubtedly in our presence. The room continued to fill with the sounds of praise and worship. No instruments, just the joyous voices of souls reborn; weeping and cries as we released our bondages, souls healed and set free; souls ready to reclaim their lives and take back what the devil stole.

I returned home with a stronger mindset than I could have ever imagined! Longing to soak up all the knowledge I could gain. I sought every opportunity I could to be closer to God. The next two months were full of optimism as I moved through this new chapter of my life. A chapter full of unforeseen hopes and promises of a brighter future. Instead of focusing on past frustrations and moments where I lacked control. I looked forward to getting to know myself again, the true me. The person that had been living in bondage all these years. Fearful to express love, scared to look weak and risk being taken advantage of. I was finally starting to realize that my fear set boundaries that only limited my happiness. "Kristina", who was created out of anger and resentment to protect me, was truly only causing more pain. In the moments that I thought I was in control; I had truly lost all control. The Devil was my master, controlling my actions and movements. This chapter was a fresh start, a new lease on life.

I started taking classes on world religion through the church every Wednesday, built a stronger connection with the choir and got involved in a Sunday morning couples group. My relationship with Jamaine blossomed into something so beautiful. We both carried around smiles of joy and hope. I no longer looked in the mirror and saw a fractured soul staring back. I saw a child of God, full of faith and a bright future. I may not have had a clear understanding of what my purpose was, but I believed every word Sister Blanch spoke over me. There was finally a light at the end of the tunnel, and I was overjoyed to be sharing it with Jamaine and our new church family. I was transforming right before my own eyes. A new woman with the armor of the Lord covering me. A stronger spirit and an unbreakable soul!

This too Shall Pass

Rushing around the house, Christmas decorations everywhere, tape flying through the air out of irritation because the wrapping paper didn't look perfect. The high ceiling of our two-story townhome echoed with the broken sounds of me trying to sing in perfect tune. It didn't take long before my laughter overpowered my attempts at singing, I sounded completely tone deaf.

My face beamed with a radiant smile as I admired the winter wonderland scene we managed to create. Matching tensile lined the staircase, tree lights bounced a beautiful silhouette off the walls, and the aroma of cinnamon spice filled our nostrils.

I was ecstatic at the thought of participating in our church's Christmas performance. This was my first year in the choir, all the new rehearsals, schedules, and planning was taking a great deal of time, but I couldn't wait to see the outcome of everyone's hard work.

Unfortunately, my excitement was plagued with mixtures of heartbreak. For the past three years, it had been our Christmas tradition to spend our holiday in Michigan with family and friends. We would pick up Jazzie and spend as much time with Tiffany as possible. Since the move to Tennessee, our time together was very limited. The new responsibilities to the church made traveling difficult this year so we had to switch things up a little bit.

Jazz flew into town Friday, December 21, and we mailed Tiffany's gifts to her. Tiffany and I chatted over the phone that weekend. My heart ached to hear the changes in her ability to speak. Huntington's was starting to take a drastic toll on her body and her capability to complete daily tasks on her own. During our last visit in July, she was unable to walk or feed herself at all, mostly using hand gestures to communicate with us. I must have taken a thousand pictures that day, trying to preserve as many moments as I possibly could. I had learned from my experience with our brother that I had to cherish whatever time I had left. When it came time to go, I lingered in front of her house, engine idling, fearful to leave her. Knowing that the next time I saw her, things would different.

Our conversations were always amusing even if I couldn't understand everything she was saying. I talked to her and my brother-in-law for about an hour that Saturday. We laughed as I told her she better be nice to her husband. Our conversation consisted of countless apologies for not coming into town, along with promises that I would see her in a few months. The phone felt heavy as I tried to block the painful memories of my father and brother from resurfacing.

She is going to be okay! I thought to myself as I hung up the phone.

Monday, December 24th, at roughly 2am. I didn't know why, but as the phone rang my heart dropped in a panic. I knew this was a phone call that was going to shift my world. It was almost as if the temperature in the room dropped with every ring. I took a deep breath and picked up the phone as my body became covered in chills.

"Hello!" I answered frantically.

"Krissi, something is wrong with Tiffany. I cannot get her to wake up!" My brother-in-law forced out as he cried.

"Okay, where is she? How long has it been since she was awake? Did you call 911 already?

"I don't know, I fell asleep and got up to check on her. I am right here with her! I don't know what to do, I called you first!"

"Take a deep breath and call 911, then call me back. I am going to start packing and get ready to get on the road now!"

"Okay, I am sorry!"

"You did not do anything wrong! I love you, call me once the ambulance gets there!" I said as I began to cry.

I rushed around my room, throwing clothes into a suitcase and hectically calling Jamaine at work.

"What are you doing awake?" He said as he answered the phone.

"It's my sister! She is unresponsive, the ambulance is on the way to get her now. I knew I should have just gone to see her! What is wrong with me?"

"Baby, you had no way of knowing something was going to happen! Please try to take a deep breath, we will get on the road as soon as I get home! I love you!"

I hung up the phone and continued to toss things around the room. Trying to gather my emotions before Jazz woke up from all the commotion. Going down a mental check-list.

Who do I need to call?

What do I need to pack?

Breath!

"Mommy, is everything okay?" Jazz said in a sweet voice as she walked into the room.

"I am so sorry I woke you up honey! We are going to take a trip; Aunt Tiffany needs us right now!"

Yay! I get to see Aunt Tiffany!" She said with excitement as she walked out of the room.

My sweet Jazzie! She was so excited about seeing her aunt. Pressure built in my chest at the thought of explaining to her that this may be the last time we get to see her at all. The lump growing in my throat made it difficult to swallow as I envisioned saying goodbye. I was not ready! Feelings transitioned quickly from sorrow to selfishness. Thoughts of Stewy flickered through my mind as I realized, just because I wasn't ready to say goodbye, didn't mean she wasn't ready to stop fighting!

Sitting in Jazzie's room, neatly folding her clothes and packing her favorite books for the car ride, the significance of the upcoming weeks became relative. We were approaching the 9th anniversary of Stewy's death. Everything seemed so surreal. With each fold of her little clothes and tiny socks I was reminded of how blessed I truly was.

Tiffany fought for roughly 14-years, soaking up every piece of life she could. Never feeling sorry for herself or wishing she had more. She was able to find the sun behind the clouds, something I had always envied about her. She did not allow her circumstance to steal her beauty, her grace, or her passion for life and living. She simply made the decision to live in the moment and love every second of it.

The seven-hour car ride seemed to take days. I just stared out the window, pleading with God to let me make it to the hospital before she died. Jamaine caressed my left leg, reassuring me I was not alone.

God I am begging you! Please let me say goodbye. I will never drink again. I promise I will follow your lead. Just let me see her one more time!

My growing grief blinded me to the promises I was making. Promises I knew I would never be able to keep. Drifting off into the dark night, clouds whisking by, only a few sparkles of star light peeking through the sky. Images that reminded me God is real and there is a purpose bigger than me. A purpose I was too consumed with bitterness to see. So, I sat, heartbroken and empty, silently crying out in pain, begging over and over again for God to allow me to see her one more time!

"Mommy, why are you so sad?" I heard Jazz's sweet voice say from the back seat.

"I am okay baby girl, just anxious to see Aunt Tiffany!" I said as I tried to hold in my sorrow, showing a brave face for her.

"I am going to draw her a picture. She loves my pictures doesn't she mommy? Oh, can we stop and get her some Mountain Dew too? Please Mom and Dad, please? Aunt Tiffany will love that for Christmas!"

"Yes honey, we can get her whatever you want!" Jamaine responded, as I continued to fight back tears.

***

As we approached the hospital, I was overpowered with an eerie feeling. The ebony sky made the night dark and quiet with a light breeze, mimicking a spooky scene from a movie. The hallways were nearly empty, each footstep could be heard amongst the creepy silence in the hospital lobby. Standing motionless in front of the elevator, I dissected each crack in the wood on the handrails, making a pattern of shapes in my mind, anything to keep me from breaking down. When we were little, Tiffany used to tell me, "Krissi crying isn't bad, it just helps seal up all the cracks in the world." She would have said anything to make me smile.

Standing there, I thought to myself, *if she is right these imperfections will be made new by the time we leave!*

I held Jamaine's hand tightly on the elevator ride up, failing to take note of the floor we were headed to. One foot slowly made it off the elevator followed by the other. My body felt as if I gained 100 pounds on the ride up. I approached the ICU desk and glanced up at the nurse, but my mouth would not move. As I looked around, I realized we were on the same floor Stewy passed away on. Just a hallway away from where I held his lifeless hand, missing my opportunity to say goodbye before he took his last breath.

"How can I help you tonight?" The nurse asked. Still, my mouth couldn't move. I stared at the wall behind her like I was looking right through her. As one tear rolled down my right cheek. Jazz grabbed my hand, noticing something was wrong.

"We are looking for our sister, Tiffany Neph, she was brought in this morning." Jamaine responded.

We followed the nurse down the hall as she guided us to Tiffany's room. Sadly, I did not need a tour.

It feels like it was yesterday when I walked these halls last. I thought.

I fought so many demons over the last four years. Trying time and time again to be brave for my family. But with the potential loss of another life, the Devil was standing in my way playing a cruel game with me. Just floors above where I was told I would never bear children, and halls away from where my brother died, I was faced with saying goodbye to my beautiful sister.

Just breathe! Just breathe!

As we approached the door, I couldn't move. Closing my eyes tightly, trying desperately to remember the expressions on her face the last time I saw her. Fearful of what images awaited me behind the door. My blood pressure shot up and my heart was doing jumping jacks, struggling to take a deep breath.

"Come on Mommy!" Jazzie was eager to see her aunt.

I forced a smile and nodded. My legs were cemented in place. Gazing forward at her hospital room door, I was hypnotized by the enchanting transformation of the door into a large wooden cellar, covered in metal locks and bolts preventing her from escaping the prison this disease had trapped her in for so long.

Jamaine gently nudged my body forward.

Fix your face! Be strong.

"Well, my sweet big sister! You did not have to put on a show to get me home for Christmas!" I said jokingly. She smiled back and moaned, enthusiastically pointing towards Jamaine and Jazz.

"Thanks for coming so fast!" My brother-in-law said as he embraced us with hugs. Sighing in relief that he was no longer alone.

I climbed in the hospital bed, squeezing myself next to her. Her body so frail and contracted, still she carried a bright smile with the most piercing green eyes staring back at me! A few moments later the doctor came in to introduce himself and explain details of her care.

"Hi, I am Dr. Jacobson. Can we step out in the hall for a moment?"

"Absolutely!" I said.

"Your brother-in-law asked me to wait for you to get here before we went over details. Your sister's condition has declined very aggressively. There is not much we can do at this time but keep an eye on her and treat the lung infection with antibiotics.

"Thanks, we appreciate you keeping us in the loop!"

Walking back into her room, such a sense of relief filled my spirit because I was there to hold her hand every step of the way through this transition. As I laid next to her, playing with her hair, my body ached, knowing deep inside she was never leaving this bed. I joked and re-minded her of all the times she saved me growing up, dying inside because all I wanted to do was save her too! Rolling on my side, face to face with her, I just smiled reminiscing about her twirling my hair, making promises to never leave when our father died. Who knew just 14 years later, I would be facing another goodbye, experiencing another heartache, stepping in her shoes, making her the same promise.

"I will never leave you!" I whispered softly.

As she drifted off to sleep, I knew it was time to have the painful conversation with Jazzie that we had been dreading. "Come on Jazz, let's get Aunt Tiffany some Mountain Dew and barbeque chips!"

The walk to the vending machine was complete anguish, as we prepared ourselves to tell her how sick her aunt really was. With each step I tried to gain my composure to say something, but nothing came out, just silence. With agony taking over my feet, and sorrow filling my soul, I was weighed down by fatigue, overcome with emotions, and angry because everything was out of my control.

"Mommy!"

"Yes, my love!"

"It's okay! I know Aunt Tiffany is really sick, you don't have to be strong for me!" Jazz said as she smiled up at me.

Still no words. I just looked down at her sweet face with a smile and nod. Holding her hand even tighter.

***

"Aunt Tiffany, we got your favorite!" Jazz said with excitement as we got back to the room.

"You spoiled brat. She did not get me anything!" I said as I gently pulled the covers back and climbed in bed with her again. Singing silly songs we made up as kids, while breaking off small pieces of barbeque potato chips and pouring Mountain Dew in her mouth. With the crisp sound of each chip breaking, my heart skipped another beat. Slowly turning my head away to secretly wipe the tears from my eyes, as I hopelessly clung onto the time I had left.

Days passed and soon my sister was nearly unrecognizable. Her small petite frame was unbelievably swollen, and her complexion held a yellowish glow as her liver was no longer able to rid her body of toxins. Her once beautiful, tantalizing green eyes were tainted with a yellow outline. They carried a marble effect, as if someone dedicated countless hours to paint perfectly precise strokes of different shades of green and yellow until an unforgettable masterpiece was created.

Knock, knock...

"Good afternoon." Dr Jacobson said as he entered the room. "Can we step in the hall please?"

"Sure!" I said as I grabbed my brother-in-law's hand and headed towards the hallway.

"I am so sorry! Her condition is decreasing rapidly, and her vitals are showing signs of cardiac distress as the fluid continues to build. We can attempt to pull fluid off but honestly, we do not think her kidneys can manage much longer."

"Can you try?" My brother-in-law asked, overcome with emotion.

"Yes sir, we will try!" Dr. Jacobson responded as he nodded his head and patted him on the back.

We gathered back in the room, head held low, all energy drained. None of us had slept in days. I was so fearful that if I turned away for a second, it would be too late to say goodbye.

She grew weaker with each passing day. Her skin had become tight from swelling caused by organ failure, all the natural creases in her skin disappeared leaving a beautiful shine. Her color was transforming from a yellowish shade to gray. While our hearts were heavy, and we sat completely powerless, she peacefully fell into a coma. All I could do was lay at the foot of her hospital bed rubbing her feet, thinking of all the things I wanted to say. My frustration towards God grew due to my lack of understanding and desire for answers. At the same time, I was thankful to God for answering my prayers and allowing us these final moments together.

The waiting room grew with family and friends, as my siblings and I rotated in and out of the room taking turns visiting with Tiffany. My mother looked broken, you saw her heart breaking as another piece of her soul was slipping away. Suddenly alarms started to sound and clinical staff ran into Tiffany's room.

"What is happening?" I shouted as I ran to one of the nurses.

"Let's give the doctors some room!" She responded as she quickly closed the curtains around her bed.

Just as I turned toward the waiting room, my mother grabbed her chest and started to collapse as my aunt grabbed her arm pulling her up. While I paced outside of my sister's room, my mother was taken to the cardiac floor for observation.

"Mrs. Quarles, may I have a word with you?" Dr. Jacobson said as he walked out of Tiffany's room.

"Yes sir."

"I think it is time for us to gather the family together and talk about next steps. I will have the nurse come and get you when we are ready. Let me get the clinical team together."

"Thank you so much, I will talk to everyone now!" I said as I fought back my tears trying to prepare myself for the inevitable conversation that was headed our way.

We all patiently sat in the ICU waiting room, no one talking. My mother was brought back down just in time for the meeting. I sat anxiously rocking back and forth in my chair, Jamaine standing next to me, rubbing my back, and one of my brothers pacing the floor.

"Neph family." A nurse said as she peaked her head in the room.

"Yes ma'am!" I quickly responded as I jumped from my seat.

"Please follow me. Dr. Jacobson is ready for you!"

We slowly walked to the end of the hall. Everyone filed into a conference room located across from the nursing station. We listened to the doctor explain the disease progression and what options we should consider.

"I know this is difficult to hear and I am so sorry I don't have better news. The stage of Huntington's Tiffany has approached is known as the "end stage". Her organs are gradually rejecting all medical interventions and shutting down. Her body's continuing to fill with fluid and she has now experienced three small heart attacks. We can try dialysis, but I have to be honest..."

"No!" I interrupted.

"I am sorry. Mrs. Quarles, what was that?" Dr. Jacobson said.

"No! No dialysis. No more medicine. She would not want this!" I replied with my head still hanging down, staring into my reflection on the conference room table.

"If the family would like time to discuss this in private, I am happy to step out." Dr. Jacobson offered.

I reached across the table, grabbing my brother-in-law's hand. "Please, she would not want this!" I pleaded.

"Krissi can decide. She knows what Tiffany would want." My brother-in-law sighed as he started to cry.

"Please stop the treatment!" I cried, lifting my head up looking around the room. As I made eye contact with my mother, I mouthed, "I am so sorry!"

Within a few hours, the family was all in Tiffany's room. Her husband was in the bed next to her. Jamaine, Jazz, two of my brothers, my mom, and I were all at the foot of her bed with other loved ones gathered around the room. As the doctor went to remove the life support, I bowed my head and held the bottom of her legs in prayer. Tuning out all the noise around me.

"Father, please give us the strength we need to say goodbye. The courage to move forward, not in mourning but in celebration of the loving spirit that you are calling home. Please allow my beautiful sister to find rest and peace in your arms. Help us to not question the things we cannot control but find comfort in knowing she will no longer suffer in pain and sickness. In Jesus name, Amen!"

"I will be in to check on you, it should only take a few hours but there is no definite timeline for these things. I am here if you need me!" Dr. Jacobson bent down and whispered before leaving the room.

We all stayed in the room, refusing to abandon her until we knew she was safe in her heavenly home. Fearful I was going to leave her in her time of need, I rested at the end of the hospital bed until her last breath. Roughly 36 hours after the life support was removed. Tiffany Adrinne Neph, passed away at the young age of 32 years old, Thursday, January 3, 2008. Three days shy of the ninth anniversary of our brother's death. I was so sad, but the gratefulness I felt for being able to share these last moments with her overshadowed the hurt.

***

I rushed around for the next few days, doing what I do best. Staying busy to take my mind off the pain. We all met at the funeral home to plan the arrangements. Everything seemed to go so much faster with her planning, than it did for Stewy. Before I knew it, it was the night before the viewing, and everything hit me at once.

The family was gathered together, playing pool in my aunt's garage and drinking. I held my drink in my hand, spinning it around and around with horrible images filling my mind. Images of Tiffany's body being prepared and embalmed. I scanned the room, watching everyone drink, get high, and laugh as I tossed back another shot of Tequila, slipping further into depression. The black cloud found a way to creep in and overshadow all the greatness I had discovered just a few shorts months ago.

God, I need you! Please guide my steps as we go through the service.

As the service started, once again I found myself paralyzed in emotional pain. I realized; I was now standing alone. My father and two older siblings are gone. I am the last, lonely piece of my father. I buried my head in my younger brother's chest. Not having the strength I did at Stewy's funeral. Tiffany's passing seemed like a final farewell–the closing on that chapter of my life. I cried for all three of them that day. I missed my father even more, forcing my mind to drift into despair.

Consumed with grief, struggling to focus, I sat lost and broken. Desperately grasping at any strength I could find. I glanced up to the left, making eye contact with Jamaine, who was seated with the pallbearers. He quietly mouthed, "are you okay?" I nodded in response to avoid causing any more heartbreak for him. Slowly sitting back in the pew, hand covering my mouth, I stared at the open casket in front of me.

"Would anyone like to share a few words?" the funeral director asked.

To my surprise, my sweet Jazzie jumped up from beside me and said, "I would like to say something please!"

Jazz pranced to the front of the room, standing boldly at the podium with paper in hand as she began to read.

"Dear Aunt Tiffany, I pray you are happy in heaven and there are fountains of Mountain Dew for you to drink as much as you want. Mommy already misses you so much, but I will take care of her for you. I promise! I am so excited that you can walk and talk now. Just like when I was little! And just in case heaven doesn't have Mountain Dew, I brought some for you to take in your casket! Mom said there will be rivers and lakes of Mountain Dew for you, so I didn't need to worry but I wanted to be safe. I drew you a beautiful picture of flowers and butterflies just like you love! Oh, I hope you can see all the pretty flowers Mommy and Nana picked out for you. You would be going crazy now at all the pink and purple in the room! We love you! Please tell my grandpa, and Uncle Stewy I said hi. Hugs and kisses, Love you always your Jazzie Phae!"

The room was full of tears as Jazz walked past the casket, gently placing two Mountain Dews next to Tiffany. Then she kissed the letter and placed it beside her before walking back to me.

"I love you mommy!" She said as she took her seat.

"I love you, too brave girl!" I said as I wrapped my arms tightly around her.

***

The music was low, as I reclined watching the clouds pass by in the bright blue sky. I am certain I imagined it, but something seemed different about the sky that day. The clouds were big, fluffy, and playful in a sense. The color of the sky appeared to be a much deeper, richer shade of blue than what I was accustomed to seeing, with pockets of baby-blue tones peeking through. Perhaps, there was nothing different about the sky at all, and the only thing that changed was my perception.

Completely exhausted from the past two weeks, I slept the majority of the ride home. In the days that followed the exhaustion continued to linger, leaving little energy to do anything. I was still struggling with my emotions and not eating well, I just assumed my body would bounce back. Soon my sickness turned into a very familiar stomach pain that I could not avoid.

There is no way! I just need to sleep!

Convincing myself that I was still in the midst of the grieving process, I washed down two Aleve capsules, cuddled up with my body pillow and dozed off to sleep.

"No! No! NO!" I muttered as I repositioned myself, groaning with each attempt to get out of bed.

I couldn't help but notice the bright, red numbers displayed on the alarm clock, it was 4 A.M. My knees buckled at every attempt to stand. Bent over in pain I headed to the bathroom, roughly ten feet from the room. As I sat hunched over the toilet I began to cry out.

"This is not possible! I cannot be pregnant!"

After the removal of one fallopian tube and ovary combined with the extreme scar tissue around the other, I was told I would never conceive.

As I tried to stand again, blood came rushing down my legs. I quickly turned, sitting on the toilet. Rocking back and forth, crying out to God!

"Please help me! I know I don't deserve it, but I am begging you! Help me for him!"

My pleading with God was much different than the four miscarriages before. I was no longer asking God to answer the "why's", no longer expressing my bitterness for being broken, or less than.

My plea meant so much more now! The pain I saw in Jamaine as I woke up from the last surgery, the agony that resonated across his face at my sister's funeral, and his unwavering desire to sustain our loving family pushed me to want to live. I couldn't stand the thought of making the doctor's prediction come true.

He cannot be put in the situation to choose between me and our child!

Bracing myself on the wall, I slowly stood to my feet, turning to look in the toilet before flushing, immediately falling on the floor in front of the toilet. Tears rushed down my face, as I looked down at a fetus floating in a bloody toilet bowl. The eyes were perfectly formed, arms bent against his or her side, and legs wrapped up in a fetal position.

I tried time and time again to just reach in and grab my precious baby, but I couldn't gather the strength. Tears filled my eyes as my mind raced with thoughts. Thoughts full of hope, healing, and fullness.

Thank you God! Thank you for showing me brighter days are coming!

Although I was still struggling with addiction and depression. I was– a barren woman– that had somehow brought forth life, albeit short-lived. God brought a piece of me to life at that retreat. A part of my soul that I had never tapped into before. I was able to identify the blessing in the undesirable outcomes.

Standing in the shower, the hot water ran down my back as the room filled with steam. Memories flashed through my head of all the times I resorted to the shower, washing away shame and guilt. This time, the shower was representing a rebirth, newness, and promise. I never imagined opening my heart and searching my soul would help bring purpose to even the smallest things in life that we typically take for granted.

Wrapped in a towel, sitting on the bathroom floor, next to the toilet I called Jamaine.

"Hello". Jamaine said as he confusingly answered the phone.

"Baby, I need to go to the hospital. I just miscarried but…."

Jamaine quickly cut me off before I could finish my sentence. "What? Are you sure? Are you okay?"

"Yes, I am sure! The baby is in the toilet. I am sorry!" I replied as tears hit the floor in front of me. Each droplet created its own puddle, connecting to the next through the creases in the tile.

"Stay there! I am on my way!"

When we made it to the hospital, we were moved into a room right away. As I laid on the bed, Jamaine discreetly handed the nurses a freezer bag that he secretly tried to hide from my line of sight. Somewhere in the midst of me getting ready to leave. Jamaine removed the baby from the toilet, placing him or her in a plastic freezer bag to bring to the hospital.

While I laid in the hospital bed, Jamaine held my hand, Yolanda Adams, *Open My Heart*, played softly on his phone. A few moments later two elders of the church walked in the room, Jamaine called them for support on his way to pick me up. My spirit was reassured of the greatness the future held, as the four of us prayed together.

In a time that most people would break down, a time where I had found myself broken in the past, I was surrounded by love and hope. This loss was proof that my God was more powerful than medicine and truly the healer of all things! This loss was proof of life, proof that nothing is impossible, pain often holds a divine purpose and things can be so much greater than what is seen in the moment!

This too shall pass!

Restoration

Whispers traveled through the halls at work and even church members questioned how long my faith would stay strong after another loss.

"Did you hear what happened to Krissi? I know right! Where is her God now? I heard a co-working giggling on the phone.

"Excuse me!" I said politely standing in the doorway of my office.

"Yes ma'am." She jerked in shock, realizing I was behind her.

"If there is something you would like to know about me, the best way to gain that information is coming directly to me. Gossiping is not cute, and God does not like ugly!" I said in a calm voice, turning to walk back in my office.

"One more thing. My God–our God– is standing right here with me. Where He has always been!" I said with a smile as I closed my office door. My back pressed against the door sliding down until my butt hit the floor.

Lord, please give me strength to accept the things I do not understand!

I started to pull away from people I once considered friends and found myself questioning the motives of those around me. Quickly discovering some members of my family and close friends preferred the broken version of me. The poison of rejection and fear of abuse which led to "Kristina" being born, was seeping back into my spirit.

I asked God for wisdom to know when to be cautious of my surroundings. I became careful about the voices I listened to, learning not to share my pain with everyone, as the devil is often disguised to gain our trust. He lures us in with false promises, a deceptive sense of compassion, and an ability to dilute our judgment and distort our understanding. Some people wanted to be a listening ear because they found pleasure in my struggle. With backhanded compliments, they expose insecurities through jealousy and criticism of the favor that was overtaking my life. Like the friends of Job, these people spoke curses over me under the guise of "counsel."

God was restoring me, bringing me back to the person I was born to be–the person I longed for before all the trauma and loss. Through all my trials and tribulations, I realized the purpose in pain. Pain brought me to the Lord, creating a relentless desire for God inside of me that would not be possible without the struggle. My trials were just my battle scars, proof that the enemy didn't win, and I was wearing them proudly. I no longer worried about the side eye glances or whispers as I entered a room.

The negative destruction that gave birth to "Kristina", became a more fruitful power. The fuel from the hurt and suffering no longer produced rage or vengeance. I stood confident, surrounded by ashes of the past burning around me, while the memories fueled my desire to not only exist, or live, but to thrive

***

The nurse looked confused. She glared at the computer screen, then at the chart, at me, then back to the computer screen. She glanced at the chart again and then at the name on my wrist band.

"Is something wrong?" I asked.

The nurse couldn't gather her thoughts to make words.

"Umm… I…. were you?... One second." she said and walked out of the room.

We had seen this before, with my first miscarriage, but this time I was not pregnant. I was just here to assess how much scar tissue there was remaining on my fallopian tube and uterus. Exploring options that may help minimize cramping every month. The procedure should have been fairly simple. A CT Angiography was being performed, this is a process where blue and red dye is intravenously inserted into the body.

For the purpose of my test, the dye was supposed to flow into my fallopian tubes highlighting the area of damage in the remaining tube. Based on my medical history, the dye would never make it to my uterus. The doctors were trying to decide if I needed a full hysterectomy or just minor removal of scar tissue.

What could be the problem now, Lord? Please give me the strength to handle whatever the doctor tells us.

The nurse came back in with my doctor at a hurried pace. She handed him the charts with a look as if she needed reassurance that she was not crazy.

The doctor grabbed the charts, flipping rapidly through the pages.

Will someone tell me what the hell is happening! I thought.

The doctor rubbed his forehead and scanned the charts again before walking over to the monitors for another look. He walked over to the front of the bed shaking his head and giving the charts one last look, and then flopping down onto the stool.

"Well, I really don't quite know how to explain this."

Jamaine grabbed my hand firmly as we prepared for whatever new challenge we would be faced with.

"As you know, the dye we inserted is supposed to show us the scale of damage in your fallopian tube. When there is damage, the dye will stop. However..." he stopped talking again to take another look.

Just say it already! I screamed in my mind.

"Well, you can see it for yourself." Shoving the image of my glowing uterus in my face, he said, "The dye seems to flow right through your fallopian tube."

"What does that mean?" Jamaine asked.

"Well, if this is correct, you have a perfectly healthy fallopian tube and uterus. There appears to be no sign of damage or trauma to either."

My heart nearly jumped out of my chest. I was cautious not to get too excited, but I couldn't believe what I was hearing.

"Wait! What? Are you saying, I can have children?"

Hesitantly, the doctor answered, "There doesn't seem to be any reason you couldn't..."

He continued to try and explain a scientific reasoning to all of this, but I had heard all I needed to hear. God had performed a miracle. My fallopian tube and uterus were fully healed and whole. With my eyes closed, hands placed on my stomach, and tears of joy rolling down my face. My spirit felt alive, and my soul rejuvenated, as my heartbeat took on a new more powerful rhythm.

Thank you, God, for restoration!

SONshine

"Oh…" I cried, rolling out of bed.

"What is wrong baby?" Jamaine said, rolling over with a stretch.

"Nothing. I am just stupid. What the hell was I thinking drinking so much? I was doing so good!"

"Don't beat yourself up. It has been a long few days." He responded, trying to comfort me in my time of need as always.

We had just got home from spending a few days in Michigan at a cousin's wedding. At first, I thought the sickness was related to the type of liquor I was drinking or the amount, but it stayed a few days after we made it back home. Jamaine finally convinced me to go to the doctor, worried that I had food poisoning due to the symptoms worsening whenever I tried to eat.

I was convinced it was just due to the drinking. It had been almost a year since I resorted to drugs to silence the voices in my head and my drinking had slowed down significantly. I made every decision consciously, every move calculated, guarding my sense of clarity, and stayed mindful of my surroundings.

"Baby I am sick because I let my guard down. That is it, I promise!" I said in frustration over the phone as we sat waiting for the doctor to come in.

"Then just entertain me!" Jamaine responded humorously.

"Bye crazy! I will call you when I leave. Love you"

When my doctor entered the room, we went through all the basic questions.

"When was the last time you ate? Do you have a fever? Does the pain get worse with any movement or positioning?" I answered all the questions, not second guessing any of my answers until she asked for the date of my last menstrual cycle.

"Umm!" I responded with hesitation. "Honestly, I cannot remember!"

"Well let's start with a pregnancy test then. Better be safe!" Dr. Reynolds said.

Dr. Reynolds had been our family doctor since moving to Tennessee, so she knew all the details of our medical history and the indescribable miracles discovered during my last scans. I impatiently sat in the room, waiting for the nurse to come in and say the test was negative. Trying desperately to not get my hopes up!

What if we are pregnant? This would be the biggest blessing ever!

Sitting on the examination table, I started tapping my foot on the footrest at 100 miles an hour, while I played with the table cover trying to relax. The sounds of the tissue paper crinkling soothed my ears. I was so deep in thought, I nearly jumped out of my skin when Dr. Reynolds opened the door.

"Well Mrs. Quarles!" She said with a celebratory smile. "I am so pleased to tell you, you are pregnant!"

"Are you sure?" I said frantically, fighting back my tears.

"Yes ma'am, I personally ran the test twice. Now there are a lot of steps we need to take. The first one will be you seeing the high-risk specialists. They will follow you through the entire pregnancy."

"Okay! Yes ma'am. Whatever I need to do!"

"I am so very happy for you and Jamaine both! Get dressed and we will set those appointments up for you!"

My hands were shaking with excitement as I tried to call Jamaine.

"Baby!" I said before he had time to get his hello out.

"Hi gorgeous! What are you so happy about?" Jamaine responded in a curious voice.

"You are not going to believe this! We are having a baby! God is so amazing!"

"Are you sure? What did they say?"

"I am still here. I just couldn't wait to tell you. I love you so much!"

***

We saw the OBGYN twice a week with an ultrasound at every visit for the first trimester. I held my breath a little more at each visit. The second visit was the most memorable. I laid on the table, holding Jamaine's hand tightly, staring into the paneled lights lining the ceiling. As the cold ultrasound jelly landed on my stomach, I took a deep breath. Suddenly the most beautiful sound in the world filled the room.

"badump, badump, badump" like the rhythmic sounds of a beating drum.

I let out a big sigh of relief as Jamaine's eyes filled with tears.

"Congratulations Mr. and Mrs. Quarles. Your bundle of joy has a very strong heartbeat!" The ultrasound tech said as she cleaned the cold goo from my stomach.

It was really happening! After so much loss, so much pain, so many unexplained miscarriages; our prayers were being answered. Still hesitant from past experiences, Jamaine and I hadn't told anyone about the pregnancy. However, after the joyous, soothing sounds of our baby's heartbeat filled our souls with confirmation of life; God reassured us this time was different!

From that point on, I was in full mommy mode. I must have gone to every baby store in town making sure we selected the best options possible. I did a ton of research, I found myself reading every pre and postnatal book I could find, searching every website available to insure I was making all the best choices for our precious miracle.

I started keeping a journal. I wrote down every little detail, from how I felt that day to what items we had already bought. I even took pictures of myself every month so my baby could see the way he or she grew. I pasted each ultrasound picture and photo of me side-by-side in the journal.

I had mixed feeling about the gender reveal of the baby. At first, I wasn't sure if I wanted to know. As long as our bundle of joy was healthy, I was going to be happy. The other side of me wanted everything to be perfect for the baby so, not knowing would make it impossible to pick out all the best things. Jamaine had been saying for weeks he knew we were having a little boy. I think he was

"Yes ma'am!" Jamaine said. The look on his face was priceless. I had never seen him so happy or nervous.

"Well, it is a good thing you want to know because he wants to show you!" She laughed.

"I knew it! I knew it all along! That's my boy!" Jamaine responded as he jumped out of his chair.

I just laughed at him as I smiled and cried. After all the trauma and pain, here I was doing the one thing so many doctors told us we would never do! Laying on this table, all doubt was gone. My heart was free of fear, pain, and regret. All that mattered was this beautiful baby boy bouncing around in my belly, and that I was sharing the most important moment of my life with the man of my dreams! It couldn't get any better than this.

***

"Baby! Baby!" I shouted.

"What's wrong?" Jamaine asked frantically as he ran into the bathroom. Responding to the sounds of my uncontrollable laughter.

"I think he is ready to make his debut, or I peed on myself!" I responded with a smile from ear to ear.

Jamaine immediately jumped into action, albeit frantic, and confused.

"Ok! Do you want to take a shower?!"

"No, babe! We need to get to the hospital"

"Right! Right!.. The hospital. Are you hungry?"

"Hungry?! What?" Slightly humored by his adorable sense of panic.

Jamaine was all over the place, and there was no hiding it. He was grabbing bags, making phone calls, trying to get me into the car. As we started to head down the road, Jamaine realized he left all of my bags at the house. He quickly turned around, "shit!" He shouted, whipping back into the driveway, and running in the house.

Dr. Makis had an entire team of nurses and doctors on standby. It was such a surreal feeling; I couldn't believe it was finally happening this time. With all the movement around me, the beeping of the monitors, and the endless questions, I should have been a nervous wreck, but I wasn't. My heart and soul were rejoicing about the fact that I was bringing a miracle into this world– a life medical professionals said wasn't possible. I was getting to show the world that God is more powerful than anything and miracles do come true!

No one could believe how calm I was, my mom asked me if I was okay every five seconds. My body was tired, but I continued to force my eyes open. The exhaustion and adrenaline mixed together made it impossible to sleep.

I could hear my mother calling and giving everyone updates in the background, as I tried to focus on the music Jamaine insisted on playing to keep me relaxed. However, I wasn't so relaxed that I didn't start to notice the increase in traffic and triple checking of the monitors as the hours passed. Suddenly Dr. Makis came into the room a little more rushed than usual, with two nurses.

"Hi honey! How are you holding up?" She asked as she made some adjustments to one of the monitors.

"I am okay. Just sleepy but too anxious to sleep!"

"I don't want you to worry but the baby has lost all of his fluid. We are 20 hours into labor, so he is starting to get a little stressed out causing his vitals to change a bit. I think our safest option is to do a cesarean section and get him out before he experiences any more distress."

"Okay! Whatever we need to do. Just keep him safe for me please!"

"Absolutely! I will see you in the operating room in a few minutes." Dr. Makis said as she gently held my hand and turned to walk out of the room.

The door did not have time to close behind her before the room was flooded with nurses. Everyone was moving rapidly, unplugging machines, my mom gathering my things, , still I managed to hold my composer. At least until I looked around the room and realized Jamaine was not there.

"Mom, where is Jamaine? Call him please, quickly!" I shouted as I started to freak out. "Mom, he cannot miss this!" I started to cry.

"Don't worry honey. We will make sure we get him to you. Right now, the most important thing is to get you to the operating room. Trust us! We are going to take care of you both. We promise!" One of the nurses said as she lifted the rails on the hospital bed and started to push the bed out of the room.

Everything seemed to happen so quickly. It seemed like the whole room was moving in fast forward as I laid still in the bed. Before I knew it IVs were in my arm, and I could not feel anything from my chest down.

"Are you still feeling okay honey?" One of the nurses asked.

"Yes! How is my little man?"

"He is doing great!" Dr. Makis said as she approached the bed. "I have some more great news for you too. Dad is right in the next room getting gowned up! We will get started in just a minute."

I was so excited. The moment was finally here! Jamaine walked in the room dressed in scrubs, with a video camera in hand and a smile across his face! There were three doctors in the room in addition to Dr. Makis, along with five nurses and two anesthesiologists.

"Are you still doing okay?"

"Yes ma'am" I answered in anticipation.

"Okay here we go. Time to introduce you to the man of the hour!"

I was staring at the ceiling imagining the way I was going to feel when I heard his cry for the first time! Jamaine was pacing the floor, recording every moment he possibly could. The procedure took a total of two minutes and three seconds.

"Say hi mommy!" Dr. Makis proclaimed holding my beautiful miracle up over the divider blocking me from seeing the gaping hole in my stomach. I have never been so in love! Before I could think, I started to jerk my body in an upward motion trying to sit up and reach for him, but I was quickly reminded that I had no movement in my lower extremities.

My frustration of not being able to hold him was dwindled as I realized he wasn't crying.

"What is wrong? Why don't I hear him?" I panicked, looking fearfully across the room at Jamaine. Before anyone could answer me, the most precious sound in the world filled the room. I never imagined I would long to hear someone cry so much. Everything about him was perfect, especially his cry!

He was more beautiful than I could have ever imagined. Light brown skin, jet black hair, big dark brown eyes that almost appeared black. His little face was so fat, I wanted to wrap my arms around him and never let him go and don't even get me started on his cheeks! As the nursing team washed him up and Jamaine recorded the monumental event, I laid with my head tilted to the left, so I didn't miss a beat! Jamaine Lamar Quarles Jr, born February 19, 2009. A day I would never forget and a moment I would cherish forever!

"Thank you, God! I will never be able to say thank you enough for this unbelievable blessing!

***

The healing process went better than expected. I felt wonderful, astatic, looking in the mirror seeing the reminisce of my pregnancy glow still shining bright! Every day was an adventure that I was excited to embark on. Until one day it wasn't.

Without warning, something changed. I found myself grieving the pregnancy process, sad because I couldn't feel him moving inside me anymore. Full of confusion and embarrassment, I was too ashamed to tell anyone how I felt. He was finally here, why wasn't I excited anymore?

What is wrong with you? You have everything you could ever dream of!

Time with my family often held some form of confusion saturated in frustration. My face was covered in a smile, displaying the expected "new mother" vibe. Deep inside, I felt like part of me was missing. Eyes heavy as my hand caressed my stomach and felt no movement, no more juggling my schedule to make it to countless doctor appointments. Nights consisting of excitement and wonder had quickly faded. My fairytale imagery of what motherhood should embody was unraveling while I hid in the shadows. Trying to conceal my pain and embarrassed by my growing depression, my mood shifted back to my mean girl nature. Pushing everyone away, drowning myself in work, and pulling my acting skills out of the closet. On the surface we were the perfect family, all prayers answered and blessings overflowing. When the doors closed, makeup removed, and peering eyes of the surrounding world were gone, my pain crept out. My truth was becoming harder to bury.

Soon my hidden secret was building so much internal pressure, I found myself screaming for an outlet. I was searching for relief and so engrossed in the idea that I must appear perfect, composed, grateful, and healed; that I didn't think it was possible to ask for help without judgment. I could imagine how the rumors would start if anyone knew the struggles I was facing, especially after such an unbelievable miracle took place.

Jamaine Jr. was only four months old when I started drinking again, trying to hide my depression even from my husband. I was too embarrassed to even tell the one person who I knew would love me regardless. Knowing that Jamaine would help me in any way he could, I still made the painful decision to be self-destructive.

I was successful at hiding my emotional instability and growing dependency on alcohol for a little over a year. I remained grossly involved in church activities, poured myself into my work, and spent every free moment I had with my little man. I even had a playpen and baby swing in my office in case I had to work over. But somehow none of that was enough to quench the flames of depression burning inside of me.

I was so frustrated with these unexplained feelings of emptiness. My inability to harness my emotions started to pour over into my work. Taking Jamaine Jr. to daycare was never an easy task. I would hold him, rocking back and forth for several minutes before handing him to his teacher. Showing up late for work became an everyday occurrence, with projects being turned in late resulting in me working longer hours. My desire to communicate with others and my ability to stay focused was slipping right through my fingers. My only joy was spending time with my precious baby boy.

This makes no sense! Maybe I should tell Jamaine! Maybe I should ask for help!"

Jamaine Jr. was going to visit my in-laws for a few days, so I thought this would be the perfect time to gain the strength to share the feelings I was having with Jamaine. I was trying to pinpoint the right time and the right way to talk to him without sounding crazy. I felt so foolish! We had been together over twelve years, up and down on more than one rollercoaster, survived more trauma and tragedy than most people experience in a lifetime. Yet somehow, I was nervous to tell my best friend, the love of my life, that I was sad. I just didn't want to let him down! I didn't want to look weak. Every time I felt myself feeling a shimmer of weakness, "Kristina" reminded me she wasn't too far away to step in and take the lead.

I finally mustered up the strength to tell him. I had a plan all in motion and was determined to get everything I needed to say out. While Jamaine picked a movie to watch, I went down to the gas station to grab some snacks. Walking through each aisle, picking something from almost every one of them, wasting time.

Stop being silly and take your ass home!

I piled all my goodies on the counter and was taken by surprise at the cashier's response.

"Oh, I remember late night cravings. They were the worst for me during the beginning and the end of all of my pregnancies. What number is this for you?" She asked with a smile as she continued to ring up each item.

"I am sorry. What?"

"What pregnancy is this for you?" She asked again.

"Oh no I am not pregnant just nervous!" I said with a laugh.

On the drive home I kept counting weeks in my head, trying to remember my last menstrual cycle. I pulled into the driveway and immediately pulled back out and headed to the closest store.

There is no way we are pregnant again! Could we be? No, I am crazy!

I rushed through the store making my selection and tossed three pregnancy tests on the counter.

"I hope the results are what you are wishing for!" The cashier said as she handed me my bag.

Mind your own damn business! You don't know me like that! I wanted to tell her. She was lucky I was working on myself!

I rushed in the house, tossed the snacks in the kitchen, and ran up the steps.

"What's wrong baby?" Jamaine yelled.

"Nothing, just going to the bathroom!" I responded as I ripped open each package forcing myself to pee. Pacing the bathroom floor, anxiously waiting for the magical little blue lines to appear.

Good lord how long does it take! Maybe I didn't pee enough!

Just then I glanced over. There it was. I covered my mouth in disbelief.

There is no way! No way!

I picked up the second test, comparing it to the first, and then the third! Hands shaking, rushing down the stairs.

"Baby! Baby!" I shouted, tripping over my feet and almost falling on my face on the way down.

"What's wrong?" Jamaine asked as he met me at the bottom of the steps.

I quickly threw my arms around him! "Look. Look. We are having another baby!" My face was beaming with excitement, eyes shining with reflections of the tears bouncing off the lights.

"I knew it! I knew you looked different!" He said with a big smile.

"What?"

"You have this beautiful glow about you. The same glow you had when you were pregnant with Jamaine!" He explained as he lifted me off the ground and swung me around in joy.

Oh God! What did I do to deserve this? I asked silently. A question I had asked so many times before under very different circumstances.

God continued to shine brightly through my darkest moments, reminding me that I was not alone and my imperfections do not make me unworthy!

***

Our second pregnancy was moving along just as smoothly as the first. Although I was still secretly struggling with my depression, my moods seemed to balance out a little bit as the pregnancy evolved.

I remained in awe at each ultrasound visit, as did my medical team! I never came to a visit without little Jamaine Jr., the nursing team just loved to see their miracle baby. I think some of them prayed for his health as much as Jamaine and I did. At two years old, Jamaine Jr. enjoyed picking out baby outfits and toys for the nursery, and he loved the idea of getting a big boy bed even more!

The day of our reveal appointment, Jamaine acted like a kid in a candy store.

"What in the world are you smiling so hard about?" I asked with a laugh, already knowing the answer.

"I get to find out I am having two boys today! Want to wager?"

"No dear! I don't want to wager. You are so silly!" I said as I shook my head and got little Jamaine out of the car.

"Okay guys. Here we go! Let's see if he or she wants you to know what they are!" Dr. Makis said as she got everything ready to start the ultrasound.

The baby was bouncing all around, I just laughed as I envisioned my two miracles playing together.

"Drumroll please!" Dr. Makis laughed. "You have another beautiful little boy!

"Is that my baby?" Little Jamaine asked.

"Yes, my love! That is your baby!" I said with a huge smile.

"Well get him out!" he demanded as we all chuckled.

"It doesn't work like that baby. Just be patient son. You will be able to hold him very soon!"

***

Because of the challenges with Jamaine's delivery. Our second bundle of joy was a planned cesarean. Dr. Makis did not want any surprises, so our visits remained weekly right to the delivery day. Everything was well orchestrated. We arrived at the hospital at 5am, we were in the delivery room by 6:30am, surgery started at 7am and I had the pleasure of seeing the most exotic, big brown eyes that looked like they had melting gold rays circling around the center, staring back at me by 7:03am.

Jayden Xavier Quarles was born October 24, 2011. I could not believe it, even with living proof staring back at me. Arms and legs moving all around as his soft cries continued to change in pitch like a radio being turned up and down, as if he was annoyed that he was taken from his cozy, warm surrounding. God had blessed me in such a remarkable way that I would never be able to repay with a billion good deeds.

It was unimaginable that God believed in someone so broken, who felt defeated most of her life. I was speechless at the thought that I was entrusted with raising these two men of God. Two men that had defied all medical belief– living proof that your story does not end when you fall. One heartbreak, broken promise, and tragedy does not hold the key to your future. As I smiled across the room in amazement, watching Jayden holding his legs straight out as the nurse held him up, and Jamaine so overjoyed he was videotaping the floor, I could testify without any question that the struggle does not last forever, and brighter days do come.

Thank you, God for my SONshine!

Darkness Behind the
SONshine

Staring at the wall in a dark room, alarm clock glowing, Jamaine sound asleep, and boys resting peacefully; I found myself once again buried in an overwhelming cloud of emotion. I tried to hold back the sound of my cries, so I did not wake them. I replayed my blessings over and over again in my head, frustrated and confused by my shifted mood.

God what is wrong with me? What the hell is happening?

"Good morning, beautiful!" Jamaine said as he rolled over and kissed me, stretching as he got out of bed to get Jayden.

"Good morning!" I responded with a forced smile.

"Is everything okay? Has Jayden been up long?"

"Yeah. I am just tired!" I responded, ashamed to let him know I was sad with no explanation to why, and consumed with the madness festering in my mind I could not answer a simple question as to when the baby woke up.

I found myself back to embracing robotic routines. My mornings and nights running together. Moments that should have left lasting expressions of joy, were lost in clouded bits of anxiety and mental chaos.

I felt as if multiple sides of me were coming alive. The happy, glowing, affectionate mother that sought to be involved every moment possible with her babies. The self-conscious, bashful woman who felt unattractive, wearing baggy clothes to cover the weight gain and surgical scarring that I believe somehow changed the way Jamaine viewed me. The mean, obsessive-compulsive woman who over cleaned everything, had to control all decisions surrounding the boys, and would notice if one pillow was fluffed the wrong way. Lastly, the speckled breakthroughs of "Kristina" that loved to resurface in my times of weakness.

Each morning, I faced a different side of me. The only side that seemed to control her entrance and exit was the affectionate mother. That side of me worked like a light switch. Every sound of the boys' voices, footsteps, or even someone asking me about them brought a smile to my face. Soon, I began to feel as if the boys were my only purpose for existence.

No matter what I do, I am broken! I don't deserve the family that you have entrusted to me Lord!

Face wet with tears, pillowcase stained with makeup, phone flashing with notifications of unread messages, and my stare was so dazed I could not even focus on the wall in front of me. I was losing more and more of myself and I didn't know how to stop it.

"Baby, please talk to me! I know something is wrong!" Jamaine pleaded as he kneeled on the side of the bed.

"I don't know what is wrong! I am lost and ashamed!"

"Ashamed?! Honey, you have nothing to be ashamed of!"

"Do you think this is my punishment for all the poor decisions I've made in my life? I know my blessings are in arm's reach, but I remain too broken to grab them."

"Oh baby! God does not punish anyone, and you don't have anything to be punished for!"

"I am not so sure anymore! I can't control these feelings. How can I hold him in my arms and grieve the feeling of him in my stomach? How can I hear their cries and laughter and be too consumed with unexplained sadness to bask in our blessings? Maybe I am broken beyond repair!"

"No one in this world deserves these babies more than you! You are a wonderful mother and an amazing wife! You are not being punished baby and you are not broken!" Jamaine reassured me as he raised me to a sitting position on the side of the bed.

"Maybe I am going crazy! I am overwhelmed with the thought of losing control. If I can't even get myself out of bed, how do I deserve those precious boys in the other room?" I said as tears dripped from my face onto my pajama pants.

"We will figure this out together I promise!" Jamaine said as his eyes welled with tears, helping me to my feet.

***

"Good morning, Mommy!" Jamaine Jr. said in excitement.

"Well good morning my sweet boy! What are you doing up so early?"

"Daddy and I made breakfast. Are you proud of me?" Jamaine Jr. asked as he jumped up and down with enthusiasm, smiling from ear to ear!

"Yes baby! I am and I will always be proud of you!"

"Let's eat!" He said as he grabbed my hand tugging me out of the bed.

Jamaine spent the next several days doing everything he could to help show me how loved I was. I did my very best to put on a smile and show my appreciation for the affection that surrounded me, but the sadness remained.

What the hell is wrong with me? My mind and body were screaming for help but I could not find the right words to actually ask for it. Even with all the miracles taking place in my life, part of me still felt undeserving and broken.

A dark room, glow of the alarm clock, and cries muffled by a pillow. A reality I found myself in every night. Trying unsuccessfully to protect Jamaine from my pain, I attempted to become an actress again. Forcing a smile, dragging myself out of bed, and half-ass attempts at cleaning.

I stopped attending church and hesitated to leave the house. Struggling to push myself more and more to add normal daily functions back into my routine.

Get up! I sat on the end of bed staring at the closet trying to convince myself to get dressed.

Damn it, that will never fit! Oh my God, I have gained so much weight!

Each article of clothing resulted in more doubt and negative self-talk. Before I knew it, I was sitting on the bedroom floor surrounded by clothing and baby clothes.

Too exhausted to cry anymore, I was back in a personal tug-a-war game. The angel and the devil on my shoulders –the angel repeating positive affirmations, and the devil telling me that I would never be enough!

It was becoming clear as day, I could not do this alone! I had exposed too much of myself, I had let too many people in.

"What the fuck am I supposed to do?!" I screamed out, loud enough to wake up "Kristina". Walls were quickly being built and a brave face being sculpted!

Breathe, we will be fine now!

***

Going back to work, I found myself walking with more confidence and determination. The Determination was not out of a desire to be successful though, it was out of a desire to convince everyone else I was okay! The false sense of confidence left me cold and closed off to others around me. With each passing day, I lost more of the beautiful person I started to become and more of "Kristina" appeared!

"Baby, I know something is going on! Please let me in, let me help!" Jamaine begged.

"What are you talking about?"

"I hear you crying at night! You are not this mean person that I am starting to see!"

"I will never be enough, will I? You want me out of bed, so I am out! You want me to look happy, I look happy!"

"No! I don't want you to look happy. I want us to be happy. I want you to be happy! Please, I am begging you!"

"I have to go to work! I love you, see you tonight!" I responded coldly as I turned and walked towards the door. Hesitating as I grabbed the door by the handle, closing my eyes, taking a deep breath, fighting the internal argument playing out in my head!

You are being such a bitch, let him in! Just go to work, everything will get better!

"All that matters is protecting what we have. Vulnerability gets in the way of strength, and we have worked way too damn hard to look weak now! I am not weak, I am okay" I said in a passionate voice

I was plagued with thoughts as I walked to the car, gazing up at the front door to see Jamaine standing in the doorway defeated.

I have hurt him so much! What the fuck is happening!

Arriving at work, I could not get out of the car. Staring at the entrance realizing just how exhausted I truly was. I sat in the parking lot, weighing out the pros and cons of asking for help. I continued to beat myself up at what I believed I was throwing away. God had brought me so far, but I was falling apart!

"Damn it! God, please tell me what to do!!" I cried out while pounding on the steering wheel.

***

"Hello Mrs. Quarles! It has been a long time. How are the boys?" Dr. Reynolds asked.

"They are better than I could have ever imagined!" I said with a big grin, quickly pulling pictures out to show her.

"Well, what brings you in today?"

I lowered my head and let out a big sigh. "I feel like I am falling apart. I have so much to be thankful for but yet I remain sad, and constantly suspicious of other's motives. I am questioning all of my choices. I don't even feel like myself anymore!"

"I am sorry to hear that! How long ago did all this start?"

"I started to feel a little off right before becoming pregnant with Jayden. Everything eventually balanced out only to come flooding back ten times more intense within days of him being born. This is horrible! I must sound like a terrible mother!"

"You are not a terrible mother! Let me ask you... how are you and Jamaine?"

"He is perfect like always. Trying to fix me! I just feel like I destroy everything I touch, and it keeps hurting me."

"Do you mind if I call him? I would like to talk to you both. I believe you are experiencing post-partum depression which can be very intense and unmanageable without the right support system. What do you say we let him in?"

Wiping the tears from my eyes, hanging my head low again, "I can't even be a wife and mother right! Go ahead, call him!" I responded in a voice of pure defeat.

"Trust me! We will get through this. I will see you back here in a few days, okay?"

"Yeap, see you in a few days!"

Later that evening, it was obvious by Jamaine's demeanor that he spoke with Dr. Reynolds. I never asked him what was said, and he never offered the details. Jamaine was unbelievably helpful around the house. He did everything in his power to reduce my stress level, his actions were overflowing in love and compassion. Such beautiful endeavors meant to create ease and security, instead reminded me that I was not good enough. It made me secretly question our relationship.

Does he love me– really love me– or does he just want to fix me? I am just too fucking broken. He is wasting his time!

"Everyone is wasting their time!" I said staring into the mirror as if I was hypnotized by my own reflection.

***

"Hello! Thank you both for coming in to see me today. We have a lot to discuss!"

"Thanks for calling me Dr. Reynolds!" Jamaine responded.

"After looking over your chart we believe you are suffering from post-partum depression and a mild case of post-partum psychosis. Both diagnoses would explain the mood swings, negative perception of things around you; no desire to eat, participate in activities, and your inconsistencies in energy. I would like to start you on some antidepressants and sleeping aids."

"Is this something that will pass with time?" Jamaine asked as he reached for my hand.

"Treating depression can be tricky. It is possible that the signs and symptoms could reduce over the first year if properly treated. We will just need to keep a close eye on things. Mrs. Quarles, do you have any questions?"

A subtle shake of my head was all the response I could give. I felt betrayed and abandoned by God once again! As we walked out of the doctor's office. I did my best to fight back tears. How in the world could I be saved, forgiven, and blessed; just to be diagnosed as crazy?

"Baby, everything is going to be okay!" Jamaine said as he opened the car door for me.

With no response, I got in the car, hung my head in despair, and drifted off to another place the entire ride home. I wanted to escape reality, secretly praying that I was in a dream. How could this loving, forgiving God that performs miracles leave me all alone again?

I began to question my belief in everything and everyone. Every time I looked my sweet baby boys in the eyes, I was reminded that God and his love are real but left questioning the lengths of his love.

Are there limitations to your love? Am I not worth saving entirely?

The internal storm I hoped would never return began to brew out of control taking me on a trip down memory lane. Sadly, struggling to fight off bitter feelings of past traumas, all met with failed attempts.

As the anti-depressant medicine started to work, I found myself once again searching for something to ease all the pains of the present and past. Anything to make me feel better, anything to protect "Blue-Eyes". With all my efforts she was fading quickly and "Kristina was eager to lock the door for good.

"Hey Krissi! Congratulations on the baby! Do you have any pictures?" Dr. Simpson said. He and I had worked together for years so he knew just how much of a miracle they were.

"Absolutely!" I said as I quickly pulled photos out. Hey, can I ask you a favor?"

"Sure! What's going on?" He asked.

"I have been feeling very overwhelmed and sad lately. Trying to get back in the swing of things has been challenging. Is there anything you can suggest or maybe prescribe to help me relax a little?"

"No problem, you know we have three kids. My wife struggled a little at first too. It is completely normal. I will call something in for you today!"

"Thanks, I owe you!"

It wasn't long before I found myself manipulating the system and was prescribed antidepressants from Dr. Reynolds and Dr. Simpson. With my little secret intact, I was able to wash away my pain and self-doubt at least for a moment in time. I was finding joy in life again. Laugher started to be genuine and tears were becoming a rare occurrence.

***

"Honey! Wake up!" I whispered, shaking Jamaine frantically.

"What's wrong?" Jamaine said, startled out of his sleep.

"Someone was in the room! Didn't you see them?" I shouted as I jumped out of bed and rushed to the boy's room.

"Baby no one is here! You were sleeping, it was just a bad dream!"

"Are you sure?" I asked in confusion.

"Yes baby! No one is here!"

"I have lost my mind!" I said as I turned away, rushing to the bathroom to wash my face.

You have really lost it! I thought to myself as I peered into the mirror, looking straight through the empty reflection.

Unbeknownst to me, I was experiencing hallucinations from the antidepressants. Hallucinations that soon resulted in me abusing the prescribed sleeping aid to relax my mind. However, I could not run from the side effects of the medicine, and I was too ashamed to tell Jamaine. I continued to play with my own dosage until the medication alone was not enough and I found my old best friend back in hand.

***

A year passed by quickly! I was trying to do anything to fight my new addictions. In 12 short months I went from being too embarrassed to ask for help at all, to taking three times the recommended dose of antidepressants and sleeping medication. All washed down with Rum and wine.

I needed to do something, and I had to do it quickly. I could feel the only pieces of me that I still loved fading away.

"You are better than this! We cannot hide forever!" I said to myself as I braced the bathroom sink, watching the water drip off my face back into the sink.

just secretly praying for a boy. All of our friends and family were making bets, the majority voting boy, even Jazz. As we turned into the parking lot, I started to get anxious.

"Baby, what's wrong?" Jamaine asked

"I am fine. What are you talking about?"

"Well, you are about to rub the material off the seatbelt so, are you sure?" He said with a laugh.

"Yes, I am good. Get out of the car!" I said laughing back at him.

***

"There is my favorite couple! Are you ready for the big reveal?" Dr. Makis said.

Dr. Makis was our OBGYN high risk specialist. Her entire career was dedicated to working with families that struggle with fertility, have a history of miscarriages, or present with hormonal deficiencies that may lead to fertility challenges. Dr. Makis and her team were such an amazing blessing to Jamaine and I. It was clear she was just as excited as we were to see our baby's big day.

"Yes ma'am! Let's do it!" Jamaine responded with excitement in his voice.

Laying on the examination table seemed a little different this time. I didn't find a need to hold my breath, I wasn't scared anymore, just full of joy and gratefulness. As the cold jelly hit my skin, butterflies started to fill my stomach and I could not hold back the smile taking over my face.

"Are you sure you want to know?" Dr. Makis joked as she covered the monitor with her hand.

As it often does, history was repeating itself again. I did whatever I could to occupy time. If I was busy, I wasn't focused on things I could not control and there was no time for drugs and alcohol.

I buried myself with work. Working between 50-60 hours per week, I enrolled myself in college and got the boys involved in gymnastics with football and basketball following quickly behind. There was no time to think, breathe, or dwell on the past. My days were consumed with providing for the kids, bettering their futures, and keeping my mind distracted. Running from myself again!

With each added activity, I tried to justify my purpose with accomplishments. For years, I pushed myself to the breaking point over and over again. Trying so hard to prove to myself that I was worthy. At the same time, I hated the person I saw in the mirror!

A daughter who loved me more than life, a husband that would do anything for me, and two beautiful prodigies alive and well. Still, all I saw was a victim, a weak and vulnerable person I thought died a long time ago.

Your accomplishments mean nothing! You are still and always will be broken, incomplete, damaged, goods! You don't deserve any of them!

Going to school activities was not enough, I had to run the school activities. Going to sports practices and games was not enough. If I wasn't the team mom and on the Board of Directors, I was not doing enough! As the pressure built, the self-doubt grew stronger, leading to more intense reliance on any substance that would ease my mind.

I second guessed everything I did, obsessing over notes for the football team and the school PTA. determined to make sure every party and award ceremony was better than the one before.

I have to be better than my parents! I have to prove to God, I deserve them!

Soon I looked up and saw multiple degrees on the wall, perfectly posed family photos filled the house, sounds of loving laughter carried room to room; still I was empty. Too many broken pieces scattered the floor. With each turn of my head, I found another part of the past taunting me, reminding me of all my imperfections. All the hurt parts of me locked away were rushing back in with undeniable strength.

The closet door was breaking at the hinge, the blanket covering the bed waved along the edges by the movement of the shadows underneath. There was no longer anywhere to hide, nowhere to run. Every glance in the mirror, every reflection I saw was failure staring back at me! I was too broken to be loved, too flawed to love myself, and too damaged to overcome the demons I fought for so long.

Why bring me this far to leave me alone! Why bless me with such beautiful joy to rip it away!

"God!! Why did you leave me so BROKEN?!" I screamed out in pain laying on the bathroom floor, completely nude. Pulling strength from something my Great Grandma Helen used to tell me every time I would confide in her.

"Dear child, whenever you feel alone and need God to hear your cries, get on your knees in your purest form and talk to Him like you are talking to me. He will listen, He

will answer. You have to be strong enough to decipher His voice from the others clouding your mind! You are a strong Polish woman, no one can take your strength, no one can have your soul! Don't ever forget how beautiful you are. You are not now and will never be a victim or a product of the bad things that happened to you! You deserve greatness, and greatness is born from pain! I love you. Promise me you will learn to forgive yourself and trust God!"

"Oh Grandma, I need you! I cannot do this anymore. I feel like I am being dismantled all over again! God, I am begging you to show me a sign. PLEASE!" I continued to beg as my tears puddled on the cold ceramic bathroom floor that I laid on curled up in a ball.

Just me and a bottle of Malibu coconut rum. I fought to pull myself from the floor, bracing my weight on the side of the tub. Each time overcome by emotion, falling back to my knees. As I rested my head on the side of the tub defeated, the water started to run. I didn't even have enough energy to lift my head and see who was in the room with me.

"Come on baby, let's take a bath!" Jamaine said as he kissed my forehead and lifted me off the ground.

"I don't deserve you! I have wasted so much of your time. I am so broken, too broken to love!"

"Don't say that... you are my life!"

"I am a lost cause. I'm consumed with bitterness, regret, and guilt. I have never been loveable. Hell, I cannot even love myself!"

He raised me up to the bathroom mirror! "Look in the mirror, I see a loving, brilliant woman. The best mother and wife in the world. A woman who puts everyone else first and leaves no time for herself. I wish I could take away all the pain they caused you. God knows I do!" As tears filled his eyes, he lifted my head towards the mirror. "Tell me what you see when you look in the mirror."

"I see a broken little girl, scared to come out. A person so destroyed and stepped on that there is no more room for repair. I am all prayed out, I am bitter, angry, and so fucking frustrated!" I shouted as I grabbed the soap dispenser and shattered the mirror. "I hate the person in the mirror!"

I pushed Jamaine away, reaching for my pill bottle and grabbing the rum. I tossed two pills in my mouth, washing them down with the sweet taste of coconut, overshadowing the harsh taste of rum in my throat. I didn't even bother pouring it, I just turned the bottle straight up. My emotions could no longer be contained. I watched Jamaine gather my pajamas and fill the tub with bubbles. Desperately trying to do anything he could.

"Come on baby. Get in the tube!"

I stared back at him with an empty, cold look. I felt as if it was someone else's eyes looking at him, while I struggled to pull myself from deep inside this body that I was trapped in. I slowly raised my right leg over the tub, lowering it into the water, followed by the left. As my body became submerged, I allowed all my muscles to relax just enough for the water to wash over my entire body. For a moment, I felt peace at the thought of drifting away. Relief at the notion that I wouldn't be in pain anymore. I would not feel disgusting anymore, knowing that I allowed another person to take my body and was too weak to fight back. Free from all the guilt, anger, and sense of not being enough. Simply free!

"Mommy can I come in?" My son's voice, like a lifeguard, reached through the shower curtain, into the tub pulling me from my watery grave. I quickly pulled myself out of the water, with his voice still ringing in my ears, I grabbed a towel to cover my body. "Yes baby!"

"I drew you a picture. It is on your bed when you are done, okay!" He said with a big, beautiful smile.

I hid my tears with the bath water covering my face and cleared my throat. "Thank you so much sweetheart! I will be out in a minute. I love you more than anything!" My voice cracked as I struggled to speak. Trying to wrap my head around all the thoughts that just took over my mind.

"I love you to the moon and back Mommy!" Jayden said as he closed the bathroom door.

I jumped out of the tub, throwing the bottle of rum towards the toilet. The sound of the cracking porcelain carried throughout the house as I watched the broken shards from the back of the toilet fly across the floor like the shattered pieces of my existence.

"I am fine!" I yelled before anyone could rush to check on me!

Holding the bathroom vanity so tight my knuckles were as white as freshly fallen snow. Glaring into the broken glass, each piece representing a different chapter in my life, I found my soul filled with courage and strength.

"You cannot have me Devil! I am a child God, blessed and highly favored. I will not fight fair. I will fight for my family and my health with all I have. Only one of us will survive this battle! Only one of us can WIN and it won't be you!"

Waging War

Kneeling on the side of my bed, begging for strength and understanding, guidance for the battle ahead and a hint on where to start, I suddenly felt a little hand wrap tightly around mine.

"Jesus, please give my Mommy the strength she needs to get better. Help her stop drinking and stop being sad. I can help if you want!" Jayden said in the sweetest, most sincere voice imaginable.

"You are the sweetest young man in the world. You make me so happy: you know that?"

"Yes, mommy I know." He answered

"Do you promise?"

"Promise what mommy?"

"Do you promise to remember that I am always happy and proud of you? You never make me sad"

"Yes, I promise."

"Me being your mommy was the answer to all my prayers. Sometimes things just happen to us that are really hard to forget. Mommy is trying hard buddy, I promise!"

"I know and we are going to help!" He said as he embraced me with the most affectionate hug.

Each morning started with a prayer, each day another piece of armor was added, but it wasn't enough. I had to close the doors and windows to my soul, evaluating those around and what their motives were. Taking note of the people who seemed to genuinely care versus those waiting for the party to continue.

No one outside of my immediate family saw the emotional breakdowns, the endless cries, the nightmares, the gazing stares into nothingness, and the empty looks day after day. I dressed the part, played the part, and won the award! On the surface everything seemed perfect, inside I was a raging sea with no clue where the wind was going to blow me next.

Everyone else still saw the fun loving Krissi that enjoyed throwing parties and being the center of attention. I was headed into the biggest battle of my life, and I had no idea who to trust, who to let in, and who should stand by my side. As my picture widened, my heart ached, my vision became clearer as my strategic plan for war was put in place. I had to let people go! I had to erase the idea of fun, protection, and perfection from the dry erase board of my heart. I had to trust God and my husband more than I trusted the drug or the bottle. I had to trust myself!

***

The world is full of many types of war, all consisting of different levels to achieve a desired goal. The art of warfare is simply to wage armed conflict against an enemy through operational understanding, strategic planning, and tactical implementation. War is hard and often necessary to protect ourselves from surrounding threats.

War was necessary for me to live without relying on "Kristina", necessary for me to live and love freely, necessary for my voice to be heard and my soul to stop hiding in the shadows. War was necessary and the time was now!

I was entering into a battlefield, involving multiple great powers, destruction and loss of life, a battle consisting of all available resources of weapons and personnel, a fight conducted without scruple or limitations. In this war I would need all hands on deck. I needed "Kristina" as the Commander in Chief, and "Blue - Eyes" standing on her right side as Secretary of defense. No longer locked away, standing strong and brave, and linked arm to arm with the best parts of myself.

This battle was not going to be easy or fun! I was preparing myself for an emotional rollercoaster. I continued to get out of bed and put a smile on my face while I was barely strong enough to get through a few hours without a drink of alcohol. I allowed the enemy to creep in and convince me that wine was better than rum or vodka. With that foolish sense of reasoning, I adjusted the *type* of alcohol I drank and claimed it as a victory.

While I prepared my spirit to cross enemy lines, I quickly realized that I was being betrayed from the inside. The enemy was living in my backyard, creeping around the corner, laughing at my frustration, and slithering in at any sign of weakness. There was no need to cross enemy lines, when I was living on the enemy's soil!

Everyday looked different, waking up with a new game face, continuing to feel defeated while I drank myself to sleep.

I was wrong! I was such a fool to think I could do this! God please, I am begging you to tighten my armor!

I was back in a game of tug-a-war, fighting the urge to drink knowing I would not be as powerful against the enemy with a clouded mind. Addiction has a very deceitful way of convincing us that one drink, one smoke, one pill will not hurt. It's just one, right? Addiction does not work that way; one is never enough but it is always too much!

I set limitations on self-love and pushed myself to the limit every day. I tried to make sure I was available for everyone else, while I continued to neglect myself. My name never quite made it to the top of the never-ending to-do list. Honestly, I never felt worthy of being put on the list. All I could see was the time I took away from my family by not managing my depression, not dealing with the monsters hiding under my bed, most importantly not being brave enough to say I needed help until my judgment and reasoning became so clouded, I did not recognize who I was anymore. There was a complete stranger walking through my home, interacting with my family, taking my place while I laid paralyzed and hidden inside the body I lost control of way too young in life.

***

Body slumped over the living room chair, wine spilled on the floor, tear-soaked pages of a Bible in my lap as I awoke. As I wiped my face, God answered me for the first time in years. A cold breeze filled the room, my body was covered in chills. As a light wind came through the living room window, the pages of the Bible flipped, stopping at Philippians 4:13. "I can do all things through Christ which strengthens me!"

I sat on the edge of the chair, slightly bent over, feeling a sense of love surrounding me. An indescribable sensation pervaded my spirit, taking me back to the first moment I prayed with Sister Blanch. It was as if God was trying to show me, He never left me. Every time I felt alone, God was trying to guide my steps. I was just too blinded by my pain and bitterness to notice his direction. So accustomed to being used and mistreated that I misplaced my own strength.

As I started to gain clarity, I realized the war I thought I was preparing for, started before I ever recognized the need to fight. I was so consumed with negative feelings and the inability to see my purpose that I didn't realize I had waved my white flag years ago. I always thought it was me against the world but could now see I was fighting a battle with myself. The enemy was laughing at my defeat, standing aside, no weapons used, and winning by default. The Devil was making a mockery out of my pain and misdirected beliefs. My story was his victory, a testing tool for his demons to prey on the perceived weak.

Still shaking from the spiritual presence in the room, I started to stand on my feet, picking the bottle of wine up from the floor.

"Here Mommy, I will take it," Jayden said.

"I got it baby!"

"It is okay! I want to help. Besides, you are not going to get better if you don't try Mommy!" He answered as he reached for the glass in the cup holder.

"Thanks Buddy! How did you get so lovable?"

"You taught me!"

I stood there, watching Jayden walk to the kitchen, full of love and life. The sounds of Jamaine Jr. walking down the steps.

"Good morning, Mom!"

"Good morning baby!"

The phone rang in the background. As I reached for the phone, I watched the boys laughing and pushing each other around in the other room.

"Hello!"

"Good morning beautiful! How are you feeling?" Jamaine asked.

"Better now!"

I fell asleep to an internal chaos but awoke surrounded by unconditional love! God was showing me that my armor was already in place and my soldiers were ready to fight. I just had to be willing to command them!

***

"Thank you for calling Recovery Unplugged. My name is James, how can I help you today?"

"Hi James." Is all I could get out before my voice started to crack and my heart was overcome with a mixture of emotions.

"Take your time. I am here when you are ready to talk. Take as long as you need!"

I tried to clear my throat and speak. Each time, only the sounds of my cries were heard. I tried to catch my breath but only struggled more for air.

"I am sorry!" I finally managed to utter with a therapeutic exhale.

"There is nothing for you to be sorry for. We can talk as long as you need. I am here to help!"

Minutes passed with only the sounds of my cries. James was so patient while I gathered my thoughts and found the words I struggled to say for so long.

"I need help James! I can't do this anymore. I am literally falling apart!"

"I have been in your shoes. Trust me, if you give Recovery Unplugged a chance, things will start to get better. Let me help you!"

James and I talked for over an hour. Walking through parts of my life I wished I could erase. Each small detail cracked a window open just a little more. Pushing through the tears, I answered every question asked. Our conversation flowed so fluently, I finally felt like someone understood what I was going through. Jamaine was always there to listen to me, but I never felt like he could understand the pain and trauma. James and the staff at Recovery Unplugged, had walked in my shoes. They felt broken at one point in life too, all reliant on some form of substance, all lost; until they decided to seek the help that I now knew I needed.

The most important decision I was ever going to make took place during a phone call with a complete stranger. The plans were final, flight was booked, I was crossing enemy lines and demanding back what the Devil stole from me. Walking to the front line of the battlefield the following morning at 7am.

***

My hands shook in terror about the commitment I had just made with an absolute stranger.

What the hell are you doing? You can't leave your family and run off to God knows where? You haven't even discussed this with Jamaine.

I wanted to pick up the phone and call James back to tell him I had made a terrible mistake. I didn't want to leave my family. I had never been away from the boys for more than a week, and even then, I was with Jamaine. This would be the most difficult decision of my entire life, and I had made many difficult decisions, but something spoke deep from within.

If you don't do this, you will never be the wife and mother your family needs.

It was resolved. I picked up the phone, trembling so hard I almost dropped the receiver.

Riiiiiingg... My heart pounded as part of me hoped Jamaine wouldn't answer.

Maybe it will be easier if I just leave...

"Hello beautiful!" Jamaine said.

"Baby... I am so tired of being sad, feeling broken and useless. I feel like I am dying! I have to get help!"

"Okay. I am here, you know that! What do you want to do?"

"I already made the arrangements. I leave for a recovery center in Florida first thing in the morning." The line went quiet. I immediately broke the silence, knowing what must have been going through Jamaine's mind.

"I am sorry I made the plans without talking to you first. This is something I have to do for me, for us, for the kids! You have taken care of me long enough! I will never be the woman the kids and you deserve unless I do this. I have to walk all the way through the pain and stop masking it or I am going to be lost forever!"

Jamaine cleared his throat, clearly fighting his own desires and seeing my need.

"You know I will support anything you want to do!"

"Promise me you won't tell anyone where I am going. It is very important to me that we are honest with the kids, but I need to shelter my recovery until I am strong enough to share my story on my terms!"

"I am here to walk this journey with you no matter what road it takes us down. I promise you are not alone, and you never have been!"

The night seemed to move at a snail's pace. When the boys got home from school, I made the conversations last as long as I could. No simple, "how was your day?" I wanted to know every detail about the day. My soul was aching at the thought of being away from them. It hurt even more knowing that I had already wasted so much precious time, now here I am stealing even more time away from them. Moments I could not make up for. Moments they would never get back.

Sitting on the floor of my bedroom, perfectly folding clothes, neatly placing everything in the suitcase. I replayed all of my decisions, weighing out the pros and cons of me leaving them. Ultimately knowing, if I did not embrace the help being offered, the mother I longed to be would never become a reality.

"Boys please come into the room. Mommy and Daddy need to talk to you!" I said as I tried to gather my thoughts and emotions.

"Yes ma'am!" Jamaine Jr. responded as Jayden walked in behind him.

Jamaine Sr. and I sat on the bed, quiet for a moment. I gazed into both of their beautiful eyes, reaching my hands out to theirs.

After staring deeply into their eyes, I finally found the courage to speak. "Mommy has to go away for a little while. I am not sure how long I will be gone but I promise I will think about you every single day!"

"Where are you going?" Jamaine Jr. asked.

"Well… you know I have been sad for a long time, and I have been trying really hard to get better but I just can't seem to do it and it is getting harder. I want to be better for you guys. I love you so much!"

"YAY! God answered our prayers Mommy. I told you He would!" Jayden shouted as he jumped up.

"I hope you're not mad at me!" I sadly responded.

"Mom! We are happy and we love you too! Are doctors going to help you?" Jamaine Jr. asked inquisitively.

Jamaine Sr. and I showed the boys pictures of Recovery Unplugged and talked about some of the doctors I would see while I was there. While my heart and mind were still unsure if I was making the right decision, the boys smiled looking over the pictures and helping me pack the last few items I needed.

***

Unable to sleep, worried about the days to come my mind raced. I tossed and turned, mesmerized by the spinning of the ceiling fan in the room. Quietly rolling out of bed I started writing letters to the boys, organizing the cabinets and refrigerator to make sure they had all the snacks they loved for school, and finally making it to their room watching them sleep.

How did I allow myself to get here? They should have been enough!

I wiped the tears from my cheek, gently feeling Jamaine's arms wrapped around my waist as he softly kissed my neck.

"Everything is going to be okay baby. I promise!" He whispered, pulling me closer to him.

"I know. It just hurts knowing I couldn't be strong enough to fix it on my own!" I responded as I gently leaned my head back, resting on his chest. "Everything is going to finally be okay, once and for all!"

***

My heart was running a marathon, hands clammy, and unable to focus, looking like a lost puppy trying to find their way home, while aimlessly reading the signs in the airport. Everything became real when I saw the gentleman from Recovery Unplugged, standing at the baggage claim. I was already ashamed to admit my defeat to trauma and addiction, but there reality stood smacking me in the face. His blue shirt with white lettering was impossible to miss.

Our eyes met as I got closer "Hi Mrs. Quarles. My name is Rick." My hands were shaking so bad as I cleared my throat.

"Hi, you can call me Krissi!"

I stood completely still, watching the carousel spin each bag around and around. Lowering my head to secretly wipe my tears away, hoping no one would see my shame piercing through my body like a sharp, two-edged sword.

Everything is going to be okay!

"I am here if you want to talk! Just a few short years ago I was standing in your shoes. Trust me. It was the best decision I ever made!" Rick said in the kindest voice.

Slightly lifting my head, I nodded in recognition of what he was saying. Knowing deep inside, every word was true. I just could not stop beating myself up for leaving my kids. I was so headstrong, trying to be perfect so they would not feel the pain I felt, but I failed miserably. Replaying each painful moment and how I reacted over and over again to see what I could have done differently. The conclusion was always the same, nothing!

My pain was deep rooted. I was much too young to process what was happening. Certainly, too young to know how to cope properly. Numbing the pain and locking the monsters in the closet was the only way I knew how to move forward. I wanted so badly to be the best at everything I became consumed. I had to be the best wife and also a successful businesswoman, an over engaged mother, and the fixer of all things. Although there wasn't enough glue in the world to hold me together.

I was determined to prove to the world around me that I wasn't broken, not realizing I was fracturing myself even more by setting the bar so high, without first achieving internal growth. I was resolute to be the best mother, showing my children how wonderful they are, constantly aiming past the stars. I failed time and time again to realize the whole while, I was absolutely the best mother because of the love I showed and felt for them, not because of the activities they were involved in or the parties I threw. What made me the best mother was loving them unconditionally, putting their needs before mine, and

making sure all of their needs were met, not only physically but emotionally. To remain the best mom, I had to
fix my soul, allow God to recreate me, accept healing and
learn to forgive. A true rebirth was on the horizon, I was
finally strong enough to let go.

Trauma Therapy

The Battle Begins

The car pulled onto a long driveway off of a never ending, deserted road. The driveway was surrounded by beautiful burgundy brick buildings and courtyards. My attention was immediately captivated by the people socializing in the serenity garden. I was both mesmerized and mortified at the fact that this was to be my new temporary home.

"Hi Mrs. Quarles. My name is Robert. I will be helping with your intake today. Can I get you any water or maybe some food?"

"Please call me Krissi." I responded as I shook my head no.

"Would you like to call your family and let them know you made it? I know from experience this can be the toughest part."

"No, I don't want the kids to hear me cry! It will just worry them and I have hurt them too much already!"

My mind went blank as I stared at the mirror hanging on the wall across from me. The sounds of people talking seemed like whispers in the background. My body was able to respond to simple requests of the nurse as she took my vitals, but my mouth remained unable to speak.

The reflection in the mirror seemed pixelated as pieces of me moved in and out of focus, being pulled back by the demons inside.

You are wasting your time! You're too broken to ever be more than a mean, stubborn, hopeless bitch!

The internal war was stronger than ever before. With each glimpse of "Blue-Eyes" in the mirror, another monster appeared reminding me why she had to be protected.

You did this! You hurt yourself and your family! This is all your fault!

My head hung down, I wiped my face and gathered the strength to look towards the mirror again. I was trying hard to focus my energy on the good and face my fears head on. As my head raised, there she was "Kristina" staring back at me; all distorted images gone, just a clear reflection of my strength.

You got this!

***

Face buried in a pillow, another pillow aligning the side of my body, so I didn't feel alone. Shots of Ativan required to achieve even the smallest amount of rest. The first 24 hours were full of tears, grieving my children and my husband. I just wanted to hold them, hear their voices, and see their loving faces.

"Good morning, Krissi. How was your first night?" Dr. Richardson asked.

"Okay... I just miss my family!"

"Missing your family is normal, your sacrifice will be worth it in the end. I reviewed your files and went over your intact notes. We have diagnosed you with Major Depressive Disorder, Suppressed Anxiety associated with depression, and PTSD (Post Traumatic Stress Disorder)."

I immediately dropped my head, trying so hard to hold back the tears.

You are the definition of a lost cause!

"Krissi! You have nothing to be ashamed about. We are here to help you; this road is manageable, and you are not alone!"

Hesitant to make phone calls that early in my recovery, I turned to journaling. I wrote down everything I felt and everything I wanted to say to my family. Trying to ensure they never doubted this new chapter was for them, for us!

With my mind already trying to process my new medication regimen, and how these diagnoses would impact the rest of my life. I wasn't sure what to expect walking into therapy. All I knew was that I was at my breaking point and there was no turning back! I envisioned a scene with me sitting on a couch across from someone who thought they had all the answers to my life-long struggles. To my surprise and delight, therapy was so much more!

I was surrounded by a medical team and counselors who all stood in my shoes at one point in their lives, eager to lend a helping hand. It was obvious that strategic planning, detail, and time was invested in my recovery. Each session was isolated to a particular part of my journey, allowing me time and an open space to grieve, reflect, and accept the events that occurred. The focus of each session did not change until I was strong enough for it to change, including the rape.

Trauma therapy allowed me to break my pain down into manageable pieces with no distractions, outside responsibilities, or timelines. I was able to cry, scream, and just be still without judgment, criticism, or fear of failure! For the first time in my life, I was able to fully process the pain and allow room for divine healing!

***

"Krissi, take us back to the day you approached your rapist. What were you feeling? Trying to really process the desired end goal!" Jada said.

Slowly approaching the center of the room, knees shaking more with every step, I sat in a chair, surrounded by other survivors and one of the therapists, Dan, sitting across from me.

"Krissi, I want you to envision being at his house except this time he is now standing face to face with you. Ask three questions, the questions that you believe having the answers to would change the course of your life in a positive way!"

With my eyes tightly closed, heart pounding, and hands trembling in fear even at the thought of being in his presence.

"Why?" I muttered, eyes still closed and head hanging low.

"I don't know!" Dan responded.

My heart began to beat faster and faster as a lump filled my throat.

"Are you kidding me!? I deserve an answer WHY??"

"I don't know. I don't remember that night the way you do. Do you really think I raped you?"

My whole body began to shake, covered in goosebumps, and I felt as if my blood was literally boiling!

"Are you fucking kidding me!? There is no way you believe I wanted this! That I wanted my life and spirit ripped from my body! Do you really believe I wanted to live in fear, never trusting anyone or anything, questioning every decision I made in life?"

"I don't see that night the way you do. I am sorry that you think I did something to hurt you, or something happened that you regretted after the fact!"

I jumped from my chair in a rage, fists tightly closed, heart beating so quickly it could be seen through my shirt!

"You DON'T deserve to breathe!"

"Krissi, open your eyes!" Dan said very calmly.

As I opened my eyes, tears poured uncontrollably. My body was tense and focused with rage, the sounds of my tears hitting the ground sounding like boulders being thrown across the room.

"May I hold your hands?" Dan asked as he reached his hands out to mine.

With a shake of my head, I held my hands out towards him. Tears continued to overflow.

"Do you feel better after asking one question?" Dan asked.

"NO! Honestly, I feel worse. I just want him to hurt the way I hurt. I want him to own what he did!" I cried out.

"This was the point of the exercise. No matter how bad you want answers and an explanation, you may never receive any of this. Certainly nothing is going to change the events that took place that day. You have to find peace knowing that you are strong, you did not cause any of this, your actions were not misleading, and you cannot control the actions of others. Most importantly you did NOT pull the trigger!"

"It's just not fair. None of this is fair!"

"No, it's not! Your pain radiates through the room. Your newfound support system doesn't even know the depth of your story. Yet, they feel your pain. He did not break you, none of your trauma broke you. You were not given time to heal and reset. This is your opportunity to finally see the truth that matters. You are worthy of being loved! You are worthy of so much more than what you have allowed yourself to experience!"

Still pouring out emotion, I just stood there in the center of the room. No words, just me holding Dan's hands trying to hold my head up. As I centered my thoughts and released a sigh, the sounds of others' cries came into focus. I really wasn't alone. I had never been alone! I went to great lengths to feel protected which prevented me from seeing my support system versus my enablers. I was so focused on finding understanding to events that were unable to be understood, I lost myself completely. I had truly been fighting a *battle within* for 28 years.

***

Each day presented another level of trauma therapy. Allowing me to dig deep into the root cause of what I perceived as my downfall. Writing soon became my outlet, replacing the voids that I once tried to fill with alcohol and drugs. All the pieces of the puzzle were finally starting to fall in place during one of my last trauma sessions.

"Krissi, I want you to imagine you are in Jamaine Jr.'s position. Picture the loving voice we hear on the phone when you call home. Replay the number of times he has told you that he is proud of you since you have been with us. Compile all of that positive energy and write yourself a letter as him! What do you think Jamaine Jr. wants to tell you? How do you think he sees his mom?"

Once again, I found myself unable to respond. Only a nod of my head as I took down notes. The next 24 hours consisted of me looking at pictures of my children, reading cards and letters from them that I brought from home, and standing in the mirror trying to convince myself to see what my family always told me they saw.

Warm smiles radiated as I thought of moments, I shared with all three of my kiddos, reminiscing on the joy I felt every time I heard one of their voices. Before I knew it, I was piecing together conversations I had with my family like putting together pieces of a puzzle. Everything started to make sense. The fight I have, the determination, the drive, the reason I get back up time and time again; it is all because of them! The words began to flow like a waterfall. My hand ached as I wrote feverishly, laughing softly to myself at the joy of it all.

The next day, sitting on the stage in front of a room full of survivors and our medical team, I prepared to read my letter. Lights shone as brightly as the hot summer sun on my face. The microphone screeched through the speakers. My hands, like melting white chocolate, grew moist and sticky as I shuffled the papers around and scanned the room. I took a moment to catch my breath, sucking down a huge gulp of air and slowly exhaling. Complete silence filled the atmosphere.

"Dear Mom,

*I don't know where to start. Things have been so differ-
ent without you home. Everyone seems a little lost. The
house is quieter, and everyone is acting weird. I miss
watching The Voice with you and having dinner together.
I miss you so much mom, but I am so proud of you for being brave enough to ask for help. You always teach us that
asking for help is not a sign of weakness, it is a sign of
courage. Thank you for showing us what that means! We
know being away from us is going to be hard, but we will
think of you every day and pray that God helps you.*

*I am sorry people hurt you, and that it still makes you
cry so much sometimes that I can see the pain on your
face. I don't know everything that happened, but I know it
must be pretty bad to make someone so strong hurt for so
long. You say something if someone just looks at us funny,
so I don't understand why your parents didn't help you.*

*Sometimes I want to ask Nana what happened and why
she didn't save you, but I don't want to do anything to
make you cry more. I am sorry you and Nana weren't
closer like us when you were growing up. I am also sorry
that nobody protected you like you protect us!*

*You teach us so many things like how to cook, clean,
and even laugh at our silly jokes. All of our friends think
we have the coolest mom because you are always there for
us. Anyone would be super lucky to have a mommy like
you, even when you are sad, you are still the best!*

*I was so excited when you told us you were going to get
help, it was like our prayers were answered. I just knew
that you were going to get stronger and heal from all the
bad things that broke your heart. I was finally going to get*

my mom back. I just wish I was there holding your hand and helping you through it all.

Sometimes when I was in my room, I could hear you crying. I would just knock on the door to put a smile on your face, because I knew when you opened the door you were going to smile back. I try not to get mad at myself, but I feel bad for not asking you to get help sooner. You would do anything for us, and I knew the drinking wasn't helping but you seemed so sad without it. I just wanted you to smile again. You always try to be strong for us. I wish I could be strong and help you not be sad Mommy!

Dad worries about you a lot. Especially when you are sad and angry! He always reminds us that you are trying really hard to get better for us. Sometimes we hear him praying too because he wants to help you but doesn't know how. If we don't have sports to keep you busy, I feel like we lose part of you. I see a figure of our mom sitting there but you don't talk or move. I knew you were in there, but I couldn't recognize you. Our mom is so much stronger than the woman that was sitting on the coach. The only time I saw our real mother is when we needed you! Jayden and I both pretended to need help with our homework just to make sure you were okay!

Please stop saying you are sorry! You have never let us down. I just don't know what happened. You seem to keep getting sadder. You are a great mom, and you always put us first! You take us to all of our sports and play catch with us even though you do not know how! You never miss anything we are doing, and you are always willing to talk to us even if you are sleepy.

You are our superhero! We pray to God every night that you look in the mirror when you get home and see the brave mommy we see. If anyone in the world can get better, we know it is you! You are the strongest, prettiest, and craziest mom in the world. Making us the luckiest kids in the world. I love you to the moon and back, Jamaine Jr."

Staring at the words in each letter, piecing them together gave me a renewed strength. So different from the "tough girl" persona I held together for so many years. I could feel this strength in my soul. A strength that gave me courage to hold my head up, accept the thing I could not change, forgive myself, recognize the beauty within, and to know just how strong I really have been all of these years. Therapy granted me the power to move forward. I no longer felt like I had to ask permission to love myself, no longer required a substance to tame my anxiety, no longer felt ashamed to express my true identity, and I had the wisdom to know what I could and could not control.

I identified a way to express all of my emotions and turn it into something beautiful, healing, helping, and lifelong. This phase of my journey helped start my path to healing! I was finally able to overcome my greatest fears. The joy I felt, and the sense of freedom that covered my body surpassed my greatest expectations. Documenting my growth, allowed me to take my loving family along for the ride. I was no longer fearful of judgment or ashamed of my past. I was excited to share with everyone and scream from the mountain tops,

"I am not a victim… I'M A SURVIVOR!

Victorious

Masterpiece

$\mathcal{F}$lashbacks of my drive to the airport just 28 days ago filled my mind as I stared into the sky. My body housed some nervousness regarding the days ahead, but I was not consumed with thoughts of hopelessness or failure like times before. I could feel the newness overflowing! I had never felt this alive, in control, and courageous without "Kristina".

Normal breathing, a melodic, joyful heart rhythm, and no sweaty palms; just laughter filled the car. No more sitting in silence, blaming myself for all the things I couldn't control, and all the things I was simply too young to manage. Thoughts of holding my boys in my arms, and calling Jazz took all the anxiety away. A new me was born and I was ready to finally allow "Blue-Eyes" to experience life. Walls crumbling down, no longer a need for security, no facade to put on, I was ready to embrace the world and be open about my truths. My story is just that, my story!

Nothing will change the events that took place, I could not go back and erase the ways I taught myself to cope as a child. My story helped create the beautiful, loving, powerful, resilient woman that had always been under the facade and was now free and ready to finally live! When we learn to forgive ourselves, we are truly unstoppable and unbreakable!

My plane took off and we soared 30,000 feet in the air, I was overcome with joy knowing I was headed home. Calming my mind and focusing my thoughts. I began to give myself a pep-talk. I started thinking of all that I had overcome to get to this blissful moment and the road that lay ahead.

I wasted so much time on false friendships and lovers, caring about what was going to make everyone else happy. There was never enough room or energy for me to heal. I had to remove myself from all the distractions surrounding me before I could understand the core of my pain.

I'm burning the walls and masquerades down. Rumors and talking behind my back will no longer affect the path I'm on. No one can tell my story better than me and I am no longer ashamed! I still wear the shit that happened to me like war paint, and I am proud of it! The difference is I have realized that all of those traumatizing events made me the woman, wife, and mother I am today. I will now have nothing but positive affirmations when I look in the mirror.

I am finally able to acknowledge that telling people what happened is not me talking shit, standing up for myself is not being dramatic or starting drama, holding others accountable is not me being bitter or vengeful, and setting boundaries does not mean I am holding a grudge. It simply means I am growing, have identified my worth and will no longer allow other's actions to set limitations on my happiness. *I get to choose my story, my journey, the path I am on, and my ending; no one else!*

I became ecstatic at the thought of putting myself first! My body was possessed with unimaginable lessons to push me forward. As I sat on the plane going through my journals, I was so thankful to God for putting these people in my life. For allowing Jayden to be brave enough to stare at me with those big, piercing brown eyes and say, "Mommy I want to help!"

My fingers brushing over each page, broken pieces slowly gliding together. It was as if a miracle was taking place right in front of me. I no longer read the inscriptions with shame and guilt, no longer closed my eyes in fear of memories not worthy of my energy. I suddenly found power and wholeness in each sentence as I reminded myself:

Don't be ashamed to cry and grieve. Sadness is the soul's way of saying what happened mattered! Holding everything in, pretending to be happy will not heal you! The pain will continue to grow until it is out of control and the reflection you see in the mirror doesn't even resemble a glimpse of the beautiful person you truly are. Tears do not mean you are losing the battle; it is simply a reminder we are still in the fight, and you are worth fighting for!

As the plane landed on the tarmac, I held my journal in one hand with the other placed across the cover! Eyes closed, I soaked up all the strength I had gained over the past month. When I opened my eyes, I couldn't stop myself from smiling and laughing inside! The war was over. I won!

Walking into the airport from the plane, I silently gave myself words of wisdom with each footstep, anticipating the road ahead!

Challenges are going to continue to walk in and out of our lives. There will always be a mountain to climb and a river to cross, the beauty is in knowing that we are capable of conquering the journey. Moving forward and remembering time is our alley (this too shall pass), will get us through anything that comes our way. Never lose sight of the blessings your life holds and what your true destiny is.

***

As I ran across the airport floor, jumping into Jamaine's arms, my tears took on a whole new meaning. I was staring at a man that never gave up on me! No matter how rocky the road got, no matter how many times I chose the wrong path, he was always there with open arms! For so many years, I fought an unnecessary fight. Searching for love and acceptance from people who held no significance in my life. My knight in shining armor was loyal, protecting, faithful, and determined to help me see the woman he saw when he looked into my eyes! The mother my children saw, the woman that deserved to be set free!

My body tingled with warmth as his embrace got tighter. I could have stood in the center of the airport, wrapped in his arms all day. I had always been in love with Jamaine, but something felt different about this hug, the connection we shared! Standing there, basking in his embrace, I realized that I had never truly given all of myself to him, I couldn't. I had never given all of myself to me. There were just too many walls and obstacles in the way. Staring into his beautiful brown eyes, a smile came upon my face, I instantly saw marvelous snippets of what the future had in store for us.

Pulling into our driveway, my stomach filled with butterflies. I was so excited and anxious to see their little faces. I slowly opened the door, peeked my head in but the living room was empty. As I quietly entered the house, I was rushed with smells of lavender and a soft breeze, slightly waving the curtains as I entered the living room. I smiled as I had flashbacks of God entering my home, flipping the pages of my Bible for me, guiding me to the path He so graciously laid out for me. Jamaine closed the door behind us, wrapping one hand around my waist, kissing me on the side of my neck, whispering,

"Welcome home baby!"

"Surprise!" Jayden yelled as he jumped from the side of the couch. "Did I scare you mommy?" He asked, as he lunged into my arms.

"Yes!" I responded with excitement and laughter as I felt another set of arms wrapped tightly around my waist.

"Hi Mommy! We missed you so much!" Jamaine Jr. said, holding me tight.

"Oh, you boys have no idea how much I missed you!"

With each tear that rolled down my face, I held them tighter. As I smelled Jamaine Jr.'s hair and buried my face in Jayden's shirt, I was laying my armor down. Finally letting go of the past, embracing the unknown, and walking in pure faith, destined for greatness.

As I placed Jayden down, I glanced up and saw my brother, Michael and my sister-in-law, Mesha, enter the room. My brother and I threw our arms around each other sharing an extended embrace.

"I am so happy you are home!" Michael said as my sister-in-law joined the hug.

"We are so proud of you!" Mesha said.

So much love took over the room, reminders that *"I am stronger than I think, smarter than I know, and capable of more than I will ever imagine."*

-Unknown

My family showed me without a doubt that I was appreciated. I felt more love that night than I had ever felt in my entire life, not only because of my family, but there was someone else in the house loving me that night– myself. As my family members began to leave, I could feel a strange dread creeping in.

Will this last? What happens when things get hard again? I don't want to go back to the hell I just left.

After walking out the last guest, I walked upstairs to find Jamaine already in the bed. I smiled and shook my head as he patted the bed as a notion for me to climb in.

"Get over here. I've been waiting a long time for this moment" he said seductively.

I laughed, still fighting the discomfort. "Let me go get into something a little more comfortable."

"Alright, but don't take too long."

I closed the bathroom door and took several deep breaths. I didn't want to hold anything back from Jamaine. I had to get my mind right. I gripped the vanity, staring at the mirror. Memories flashed through my mind of the many traumatic moments I experienced in this very bathroom. I could still hear the sounds of the mirror I shattered into a thousand pieces just days before going to therapy.

"No!" I whispered to myself. "I will not go back there. I'm no longer that victim who had no control of her life. No matter what, I will fight for my freedom. I'm never going back."

I looked back up with a new determination. No glances down or away, I was eye to eye with my reflection. I didn't see "Kristina", I didn't see "Blue-Eyes" and I didn't see a victim. I saw ME in all of my splendor. All that I had endured created something brand new. *A beautiful disaster was turned into a one of a kind masterpiece!*

With one deep sigh, all of the shattered pieces of my life were merged together, no more scattered memories of the past haunting me, no more devilish lies deterring my journey. Just my bright blue eyes and dimples filled the mirror, and the warm sensation of love and victory covered the room!

My life begins now!

Wisdom Beyond Measure

*M*y growth has allowed me to embrace being different and understand fully that my brokenness is beautiful. My creativity makes me capable, and my uniqueness makes me one of a kind. I no longer wish for those who hurt me to feel my pain. I pray that someday they are also able to look in the mirror and face the demons that hold them captive.

I pray each and every day that I have made the right decisions for my family—decisions that make Jamaine and our children proud, decisions that honor the memory of my older siblings and our father. Most importantly, I look in the mirror everyday knowing I am proud of myself. I realize my pain and tragedy served a bigger purpose. I am a beautiful, powerful woman, wife, mother, and child; born out of a tragic disaster. Every movement and decision I make going forward will be made out of purpose and will hold the reward of true happiness and pleasure.

It has taken me a long time to realize that I don't need to apologize for being myself, if the people around me don't like the person I am then I need to pick better surroundings. I rejoice knowing that I burned all the pieces of the broken me down. I am transparent with those around me, and honest with myself about who I am, the person I desire to be, and the work I have left to do. I don't pretend to have it all figured out, but I will not settle for less than what I deserve! My transparency allows me to hold my head up high and give all the facts so when people who don't have my best interest at heart choose to chime in, they have the entire story.

Growth is a beautiful journey, understanding, forgiveness and acceptance just makes it bloom into something breathtaking.

The strongest people are not the ones that display their strengths for the world to see! We are the ones that WIN the battles that very few realize we are in!

-Unknown

www.ingramcontent.com/pod-product-compliance
Lightning Source LLC
Chambersburg PA
CBHW070911120626
46546CB00001B/216

* 9 7 8 1 9 5 6 4 6 9 3 1 8 *